Hutchison House Seminar
October 1978.

A GENTLEWOMAN
IN UPPER CANADA

A GENTLEWOMAN
IN UPPER CANADA

THE JOURNALS OF
ANNE LANGTON

Edited By
H. H. LANGTON

CLARKE, IRWIN & COMPANY LIMITED

Toronto, Vancouver

Copyright, Canada, 1950
by CLARKE, IRWIN & COMPANY LIMITED

First published in paperback format 1964

ISBN 0 7720 0200 2

7 8 JD 75

Printed in Canada

PREFACE

In the second quarter of the 19th century a wave of immigration from the British Isles swept over Upper Canada. The Canada Company was incorporated and received a grant of land for settlement in the western part of the province. Under the able and energetic management of John Galt, the Scottish novelist, roads were cut through the forest to connect the towns founded for marketing purposes. The prosperity of Guelph, Sarnia, Galt, and even London dates from those beginnings in 1827. Another district picked out for settlement from England was called the Newcastle District and embraced what is now contained in parts of the Counties of Northumberland, Durham, and Peterborough. The cluster of small lakes to the north of Peterborough, interconnected and discharging their waters through the Otonabee River, was an attractive feature of this district, besides being a guarantee of ample rainfall for farming purposes. Peterborough was selected as the central town of the Newcastle District, and was so named after Peter Robinson, who had been largely instrumental in bringing a number of families from Ireland to settle on the land in the neighbourhood. This settlement was carried out a few years before John Galt founded Guelph for the Canada Company and made his roads through the forest to Lake Huron. The Newcastle District had the advantage of abundance of water communication, and few roads were needed except to connect lakes between which the river from one to the other was too shallow or too rapid for boats and canoes.

It may have been the attraction of these lakes, with the prospect of some amusement in fishing and boating, that induced so many young men of well-to-do English families to make their experiment of settling in the neighbourhood of Peterborough. It is certainly remarkable that a great part of the shore of Sturgeon Lake was in the possession of settlers who, in those days, would be called gentlemen, some of them University men, and a hundred years ago a University degree was the usual introduction to the Church, the Bar, or the House of Commons. The following sentences from one of John Langton's letters to his father bears this out. He is describing his first visit to Sturgeon Lake and its neighbourhood.

There are several reasons which induce me to give a pre-ference to the Newcastle District. It is the most English of all the districts—There is not that want of water which has caused such great loss in many of the inland townships; instead of being shut up on all sides by forests you may obtain a healthy, airy frontage to some of the numerous lakes . . . and, lastly and principally, it has an extent of in-ternal navigation unparalleled in any part of the world I should think.

Again, in a letter to a friend written about the same time (August 1833), he says:

On Sturgeon Lake you will find six settlers. Certainly this is not many, but then four of them have been at an University, one at the Military College at Woolwich, and the sixth, though boasting no such honours, has half a dozen silver spoons and a wife who plays the guitar.

In the year 1833, therefore, John Langton had decided to try his hand at farming in the colony, in preference to what might be a long and unremunerative period as a junior barrister in England, and he established himself on the east-ern side of that arm of Sturgeon Lake at the end of which the town of Fenelon Falls is situated. To the south of his land lay the peninsula known as Sturgeon Point. He had friends to the north of him, Wallis, Jameson, Dennistoun. On the south side of the lake, also at its western end, were McAndrew, Macredie, and McCall, with all of whom he maintained close and lasting friendship. At the eastern end of the lake, near what is now Bobcaygeon, were Need, Atthill, D'Arcos, Sawers and Fraser; with these he maintained friendly relations also, but he came in contact less frequently with them than with the others at his own end of the lake. Later arrivals who will be mentioned in some of these letters were Mossom Boyd, subsequently identified with Bobcaygeon, and the family of the Reverend James Dunsford, whose house, the Beehive, is still in occupation a few miles west of Bobcaygeon on the north shore of Sturgeon Lake.

John Langton's immediate family, whom he had left behind in England, consisted of father, mother, sister, and the unmarried sister of his mother who lived with them. An elder brother, William Langton, was established as manager of a private bank in Manchester. The father, Thomas Langton, had carried on a prosperous business as commission house for Russian products, but the years of commercial depression after the Napoleonic wars had diminished his resources, and he was living, at the time of John's emigration to Canada, in modest retirement on the outskirts of Liverpool with the above mentioned female members of the family.

From the time of John Langton's arrival in the New World he made a practice of writing copious letters to his father, describing all his experiences and giving all his impressions of the country and its inhabitants. Some of these letters have already been printed in a volume entitled *Early Days in Upper Canada*[1] published in 1926. One effect of these more or less enthusiastic letters from Canada was to arouse in Thomas Langton a strong desire to see this new country and share some of his son's experiences. He had an adventurous disposition and was not without intimate know-

[1] ed. W. A. Langton. The Macmillan Company of Canada Ltd.

ledge of other countries, thirteen or fourteen years of his early manhood, from 1787 to about 1800, having been spent at Riga, and five later years, from 1815 to 1820, in Switzerland and Italy. This later period of foreign travel had been largely devoted to the education of his children. They all went to schools in Switzerland, John being an inmate of Pestalozzi's establishment at Yverdon. At Rome again, where the family spent two winters, education was not forgotten, and Anne received there the foundations of her training in painting, to which art she was devoted for the rest of her life.

As most of the letters in this volume are from Anne, it might be well to give some account of her. She was a year or two younger than William and four years older than John. She never married, and became the much loved and appreciated Aunt Anne of two families of nephews and nieces. After the deaths of her mother and aunt in 1846 she returned to England for a series of long visits to her brother and other relations and friends in that country, but in spite of inducements held out by William to remain as a permanent member of his household she decided that her real home must be with John and his young family in Canada. So, except for occasional journeys to England to see her brother and his sons and daughters there, she remained in Canada from 1850 as a member of John's household for the rest of her life, and died there in 1893 in her 89th year. It has been mentioned that she received lessons in art during the travels of her family. Her artistic talent was very marked and she was always an indefatigable sketcher. But her early training was as a miniature painter. In those early days of the 19th century before daguerrotypes and photographs had been invented the only family memento of a father or mother was the miniature. So Anne practised her art as a miniature painter later in England partly as a means of livelihood, and many likenesses of relatives and friends from her brush are still in existence. Another branch of miniature painting was copying celebrated pictures, and there are also extant many miniature copies made by Anne of paintings by Italian artists such as Guercino and Correggio, the popular painters of that generation. It may be added that Anne was afflicted with deafness at an early age, which became very marked in later life, and this doubtless assisted in developing her interest in what appealed to the eye. There are many passages in the letters which show how sensitive she was to natural beauty and even to atmosphere effects, even as conditioned by the smoke of forest fires. Nevertheless, as long as her hearing permitted she was devoted to music, and in Peterborough she was the organist and choir director of the Anglican Church from 1852 to 1855, when she, along with her brother and his family, moved to Toronto.

Thomas Langton, then, finding retirement in a Liverpool suburb with reduced means to be rather dull, proposed to his family that they should follow the younger son to the New World. Letters passed between father and son on the subject, the latter making all the reasonable objections, such as his father's age and liability to serious illness, with no doctor nearer than Peterborough, almost a two days' journey away from Sturgeon Lake under the most favourable circumstances. But of course it was a delightful prospect to have the companionship of his father, mother, and sister and he wrote that he was sure he could build them a house in which they might be comfortable in the coldest winter weather, so the objections were waved aside and the family prepared to emigrate. They were leaving behind in England the elder son, William, who with his wife and growing family lived in Manchester, and to him and his wife all the correspondence contained in this volume was addressed. With great foresight he preserved it, and from his heirs it has been transmitted to the Canadian members of the family, and by them selections, such as might be of interest to later generations, are published in this volume and its predecessor, *Early Days in Upper Canada.*

A GENTLEWOMAN
IN UPPER CANADA

1834

Extract from a letter from JOHN LANGTON *to his father* THOMAS LANGTON *dated from Blythe Cottage, Fenelon, July 28, 1834.*

The only subject which I have now left to enlarge upon is your coming out to Canada. You will probably have heard from Hugh Hornby, to whom I wrote a very hasty letter the other day, that I have made up my mind upon the subject. The fact is that you gave me a month to consider it well, and I have taken six before I could come to a determination. Though I said nothing about it in my letters, simply because I could not speak decisively, I was decided upon one point—that your emigration should not take place this summer. Those who have not seen the hurry and confusion of a first year in a new settlement, with twenty things to be done at once and neither hands nor time to do one effectually, cannot of course exactly comprehend the state of affairs; but you will easily imagine that if in addition to this I had to make preparations for your reception the work would have been doubled on my hands and nevertheless I should have found it difficult to have made you at all comfortable before winter. Now, however, I have a good clearing beforehand; my own house and buildings are, or soon will be, sufficient for the present, and all the other nameless things which have to be done on first settling will no longer occupy my attention; but above all I have now seen enough to authorize me in promising that you will have to encounter no unbearable fatigues or privations, and I have gained experience of what is to be done and how it is to be done for your accommodation, which will save me from doing many things twice over. I can now therefore say that I advise your coming out to me, and that next spring I can be ready to receive you. For myself I never did doubt that your company would add much to my comfort, and I have seen enough of what is done, or rather what is not done, during my necessary absences to be well aware how much better the farm would go on were there somebody about the place to act as viceroy. However, it is not on my own account that I approve of your scheme; comfort I have learned to do pretty well without, and, in due time, a viceroy may perhaps be found. I do not know how I can promise you greater happiness here than you might have at home, only that it seems to be your wish to try the change. I certainly never should think of proposing to anybody at your time of life to come to the backwoods unless a large family were the inducement, but the proposal comes from you, and all I have to do is—to tell you what you have to expect, leaving you to determine whether you will make the sacrifice.

To you then in the first place I must address myself and tell you what *you* will miss here. You will miss society of which you are fond, at least you will find no one of your own age with whom you would like to associate much, and anything in a literary or scientific way is a still rarer occurrence; but you will meet with some very agreeable, well informed *young* men, some of whom I know you will like, and a quiet rubber or a game of chess with occasional varieties will not be wanting. Then I am afraid of our hot summers (the thermometer 95° in the shade last Saturday) and our cold winters, minus 17° at Peterboro'. Only one thing more strikes me with regard to you; it is a matter of slight importance in itself but it recurs every day—viz., eating. Next year things will be much improved in this respect and my mother's culinary knowledge will do more. But do what you will, for a year or two you will have often to dine on salt pork. These will be your trials, and, if you can get over them, I doubt not that, with superintending improvements, experiments on the farm in a small way, botany, a book and a map, you will get through life very comfortably. It occurs to me that, as a consolation, rheumatism is almost unknown in this country, our cold being almost always dry cold; but again—the distance from medical advice, should your cold complaint return, is a matter for deliberation, and I should say especially as to its possible return on the voyage.

And now my dear mother—for society, salt pork and cold I know you do not care, and the heat is so tempered with breezes that I do not think much of that. Thunderstorms we certainly have frequently in summer, but with that exception I do not dread the climate for you; if you could overcome the voyage out, I know of nothing to annoy you much here except the servants, and so convinced am I that you never could agree with them that I should make it a *sine qua non* that Anne take the whole housekeeping department. I should assign you each a separate office. My father of course would be my adviser and in my absence the *alter ego;* to you should be exclusively left the duties of beautifying the house and garden, no sinecure on a new farm; Anne must be Prime Minister in the Home department, and Aunt Alice, for, if you come, she must accompany you, shall reign paramount in the pigstye, poultry yard, etc., and shall be my Master of the Wardrobe. To Anne I need say nothing as *she is determined to come out* and as, with the assistance of the Swedish stove, she may be as content as at Bootle. To Aunt Alice I need only say —that my mother will be there; her presence is more conspicuously wanted than that of any of you—in the shape of trousers rent, buttons missing or strayed, and several heavy casualties lately in the poultry yard.

1835

Extract from a letter from JOHN LANGTON *to his father dated 21 July, 1835.*

Upon the subject of Richard Birley it is very difficult to advise. I would recommend any person in his situation to purchase a partially cleared farm but not one in full operation,—say a farm with 20 acres that have been cropped and laid down in grass, and such a farm, with house on it which might serve for a kitchen or for the workmen, might I think be got within 5 or 8 miles of a market for £150. £50 more must be allowed for building a house to accommodate his family and for a barn. Observe that these must both be log buildings quite of the common kind. He should then have for £200 his house and land; the grass would at once enable him to keep oxen and a cow or two, and he might go on yearly chopping and adding to the extent of his farm and at the end of 3 years he would be able to break up his grass and commence farming upon a more regular system; but he must consider that the fitting up of the house for his family would cost a good deal, and, for the first year at any rate, he must calculate upon having to buy all his provisions; the wages of a good man and his keep would very easily amount to £50 a year, and, notwithstanding all that Mr. Pickering may say to the contrary, in 9 years out of 10 the first crop will not pay for the expenses of clearing his new land. Then there are several years to wait and very serious expenses to be met before the whole farm will be under proper cultivation and producing adequate returns. In my opinion a man with a family, unless he have boys old enough to assist him and unless he is determined to work hard himself,—and indeed determined that he and his boys should do the main part of the work themselves—I say unless a family man be so situated he should not attempt to settle on a farm in Canada with less than £1000 and even with that he must use great economy. A single man, even upon an uncleared farm, where of course you have longer to wait before the farm is fully productive, may soon get far enough to live at a very small expense, but for a family man I would decidedly recommend partially cleared land. . . . I cannot conceal from myself that had I gone upon such a farm as I am describing instead of going upon Sturgeon Lake should in all probability have been richer than I am by £200 or more.

1837

Extract from a letter from ANNE LANGTON *begun on a packet ship* INDEPENDENCE *to* WILLIAM LANGTON *in Manchester.*

Wednesday, May 31, 1837.

I will give you a few hints in case you or any of yours cross the Atlantic. Bring a small mattress with you, for the aching of the bones when obliged to toss upon a hard, uneven surface for some days is no trifling inconvenience. My cold may have made mine more tender than usual. In the next place, bring a few basin cloths, for one is apt to look upon one's wash-hand basin with perpetual mistrust. Do not be quite dependent upon the packet's library for reading. I am glad that we are not so. There are odd volumes, pages torn out, and the key sometimes not forthcoming. But I should strongly recommend avoiding a crowded packet-ship and therefore one of great repute, or perhaps a packet-ship at all. A person should have health and spirits to stand the noise, the confusion and the merriment. Go where you will, there is no quiet except on a day like this, when the wildest appear subdued. There is certainly a great advantage in being able at all hours to call for anything—gruel, tea, lemonade, sago, or anything you can well think of. I do not say all good of their kind; our tea, for instance, is neither good nor hot; coffee better. Your dinner when brought to you may often be cold, and when your appetite is most delicate a great, big, fat slice may be sent to you. These evils would diminish when you could sit at table, but the dreadful length of the meal would be worse. I said to one lady, who had been at the table at least two hours, "I am sorry for you having had such a tedious sit." "Oh, I like it," said she, "and I have been eating all the time." The dinner benches having backs you cannot move without disturbing several, unless you can get to one end. I wish these backs were on some of the stools, for unless you are lucky enough to get one of the sofa corners there is no rest for the head except such as the elbow and hand can afford, and rest for the head is often indispensable on board a ship. We have great comfort from the spare pillows.

I generally contrive to perform the great task of dressing myself in time for breakfast, which meal appears about nine o'clock. The transatlantic ladies eat cold and hot meat, fried or pickled fish, or oysters, to this first meal, which seems with them a substantial one. A cup of coffee and a cracker is generally mine. The eggs are dubious, and your basket was a most wise and acceptable addition to our sea store on my father's account.

Wednesday, June 7.

Yesterday, when our spirits were high, a lottery was set on foot—a usual amusement, I find, on these voyages. The tickets, 10s. each, are marked, each with six given hours of a given day, between the 17th and 25th of June, and whoever has drawn those hours on which the pilot comes on board will have won the purse—the first ticket including all preceding days. This was immediately sold by auction again for £3;10s, and as the wind and weather may change the expectations regarding our arrival, more buying and selling takes place, and the interest and amusement are kept up.

New York, Tuesday, June 20.

On Monday morning, the 19th, I accompanied my father to the ship to superintend the examination of our baggage. It was a tedious, fatiguing, and patience-trying affair, and I could not help thinking we were more narrowly scrutinized than others, though nothing in the end was objected to. Shall I give you a chapter on American hotels? I think not—this is more particularly a journal of the sea. Suffice it to say, that I find reason in some respects to rejoice that we have been hardened by previous travel.

June 29.

Yesterday my father and I dined at Mr. Walker's, to whom Mr. William Rathbone had introduced us. We had a very pretty drive of ten miles to a very pretty place, looking upon the East River, as they term the water dividing us from Long Island. As we came home at night the fireflies were as beautiful, though not quite so numerous, as I have seen them in Italy. We were entertained likewise by the musical notes of the American frog.

The family was detained in New York by Mrs. Langton's illness, but finally, early in July, continued the journey, a detailed account of which is given in the following extracts from Mrs. Langton's journal sent to her son in England.

Extracts from MRS. LANGTON'S *journal sent to her son* WILLIAM LANGTON.

I had made a little journal, or rather diary of my feelings when first embarking on our awful voyage—and when I could employ my pen during it; but when I looked it over it was such a melancholy catalogue of sufferings and sensations produced by sea-sickness that I thought it better torn and destroyed than distressing dear William with a perusal of it—and I wish, now that we are once more on *terra firma,* to banish what is past from my thoughts, and, if I could, the feelings of my last sight and touch of my first-born, but the stunning sensation can never be forgotten, and my feeling when the ship cleared the pier-head must ever remain as long as memory lasts. It was a call on all my energy and resolution to support an appearance of composure. What a relief would tears have been! I often found myself thinking that I shall tell William, or this I shall remark to Margaret—and heavy indeed has it fallen when reality told me we should never meet again.

We arrived at New York on the 18th of June—22 days from embarking. I had flattered myself by proper management I might be relieved from the distressing stupor in my head and binding deafness, but medicine, blisters, etc., failed of success—fever came on and I really thought I should never leave New York. Being somewhat better for a day or two, and it being the opinion of Dr. McNeil that easy travelling and short days' journeys would do me good, we decided to proceed forward, which we are all anxious to do, and left our clean and airy rooms at the Mansion House in Broadway on the 3rd of July after staying just a fortnight in New York. We were all impressed with the beauty of the scenery on the banks of the river as we approached; the Bay too is considered fine, but it did not particularly strike me. . . .

3rd: Embarked in the Steam Packet which goes to Albany, but we determined to stop short half-way at West Point, a beautiful station, and rest there a day or two. The banks are very fine—some striking rocks and palisades, indeed all are fine. The river too (the Hudson) we admired, the Point has beautiful scenery. The Hotel commanded it on all sides, but we were taken aback by hearing we could only have one bedroom, though two had been spoken for the day before. The house quite full, many military, as tomorrow is the anniversary of American Independence, always observed, and this place is where the military college is situated. The mountains are fine which surround the view of the river. T.L.[1] thinks it one of the most lovely spots he has ever seen: its view offers Anne some sketching: a most numerous public table. T.L. got a small room and we did very well with our two beds. The weather not very hot.

4th: Company kept coming in last night, every room and passage full with temporary beds. The morning was fine and I had had a tolerable night. There was a sort of review of the young military. They went to church where there was a prayer and a hymn, and then one of the youths mounted the pulpit and read the Articles of their Independence—loudly

[1] Her husband, Thomas Langton.

applauded—afterwards a sort of oration was made, which our party thought rather long but which elicited the strongest applause. A dinner followed and thus ended the festivities of the day.

5th: I felt better this morning than I have done since before my voyage. T.L. and I had a walk about this lovely spot but rain came on which has confined us all the afternoon. We saw the fire-flies this evening for the first time since Italy, but not very numerous.

6th: Not a good night and my hopes of yesterday somewhat dampened. My head very indifferent, with noise oppressive and deafness very distressing, but anxious to proceed if only a little way. We embarked for Albany in a New York Steam Packet about eleven. A comfortable rocking-chair was placed near the end of the upper deck; I had plenty of air and found it not at all too hot, and by being on the upper deck avoided the crowd of company who were chiefly below. I remained perfectly quiet during the 7 or 8 hours of our passage. We found the Eagle at Albany very near where we landed—a most comfortable-looking house, the rooms very spacious, beds with beautiful linen, and after lying down to rest my poor head I enjoyed a cup of tea with some fresh strawberries. We had not dined on board, therefore were glad of some refreshment. The Hudson continued fine, the banks less bold but richly wooded down to the water. Many beautiful elegant-looking villas with openings down to the river showing their light fronts, which reminded us of Italy. They were all of pure white. The woods were of the freshest green and appeared not of old growth. We stopped at many towns to take up or set down passengers—at all a busy shipping appearance. Several towing steamers passed which appeared to have on every side of them different sized vessels and crafts, most of them bulky concerns; we are now at Albany.

7th: After breakfast I took a walk in the town, a very considerable one. The public buildings are handsome, we saw two of marble, one of fine white, the other of a sort of Alfresno, and I believe some others also were of marble—this is the capital of the State of New York. At the Inn we met with Irish servants who had been some years in the same house; the waiter was quite a young man but had been there seven years. This gives one some hopes that we may be fitted with some good Irish girl, but the accounts of the state of servants were very bad. T.L. decided we should only go for about[1] on the railway, it would shorten the journey to Utica for tomorrow.

8th: I had not a bad night but felt scarcely up to 6 hours' railway travelling, but we set out about half-past nine and were so fortunate as to have the carriage to ourselves. The scenery in some parts is magnificent with the interminable forest which now becomes visible and reminded us that we are in the New World—the stumps remaining in some of the cleared ground told us what we were to expect at Blythe. They have a sad disfiguring appearance. We arrived at Utica about two, and I have borne the six hours better than I expected—the sparks from the engine kept us on the alert, and poor Anne! From her gingham never having been washed I suppose it was more tinderish than my sister's and mine. It was sadly burnt; at times with all our care it was in a flame and the damage almost precludes repairing. It was too warm to keep the windows closed to prevent this annoyance—but we have not suffered inconvenience from the heat—the thermometer not being more than 82. The day was very favourable, a clear sky but a nice breeze—a number of neat villages on the route. Our Inn Bagges a very good one—went in to dinner for the first time to the public table, a very quiet one and not very numerous—we have now generally ices—strawberries seem the only fruit. I had a walk in the evening, there were some good streets and numerous good shops. The trees are not yet large but there will soon be good boulevards. We went to look at the boat which is to convey

[1] Word omitted in the original. They went to Schenectady and spent the night there.

us tomorrow on the Erie Canal to Syracuse. They are not so large, at least the cabins, as the Booth Boats—it felt close and hot but Madame was promised a mattress and the best places. We shall be at least 12 hours on the passage if we go to Syracuse, but we may, if we find it desirable, stop at some of the towns on the banks.

9th: I had not a very good night, but no hesitation in breakfasting at 7 a.m. and we were in the boat at half-past. Very few passengers appeared—no females. We had the Ladies' Cabin to ourselves with only the exception of the stewardess, a conceited vain girl who employed herself chiefly in looking at herself in the glass, arranging her hair (which was certainly very neat in a Jane Cordwell style, only auburn), touching her face with some beautifying thing and removing every little impurity of the skin—at least examining it to detect any. She amused me, but is the most indolent sleepy being, yet certainly rather a fine-looking girl. The scenery is very interesting, being chiefly through magnificent woods, I might say forests. I felt squeamish all day, but as we had no addition to our cabin we determined to go on through the night, which would be much gained; therefore we did not stop at Syracuse where we arrived about nine— and soon after the Cabins began preparing for the night. The seats opening in our Cabin, with mattresses laid on them, made comfortable beds—we did not undress more than putting on night caps and dressing gowns. We had some locks to pass which occasioned noise and some disturbance —but I believe we had all some comfortable sleep.

10th: I was ordered to rouse soon after 5 so that the beds might all be stowed away and the cabins arranged for breakfast. Yesterday was Sunday—it was spent in a *little* reading but more lounging and looking through the newspapers— to-day will be equally idle. We have some books and we read, we regard more the magnificent forest scenery on the banks and repose much on our mattresses. We arrived at Rochester about 9—very disagreeable disembarking at night with our various packages; the Eagle a very large Hotel.

11th: Breakfasted at the public table at seven; set out on a railway to join the Packet on Lake Ontario for the distance to Lewiston. As we have the wind against us it will occupy 14 hours. Dined at the public table a large party—the accommodations very good, very superior to English Packets —sat most of the day on the deck of the ship. It was very cool, had the bank on the left in view all day, occasional little clearings but not many. We arrived at Lewiston nearly in the dark and the hotel was at some distance from the landing. I should remark that the town of Rochester is very considerable and with handsome streets, though in 1812 it was only a few houses in the wilderness.

12th: Breakfasted in my own room, felt somewhat fagged and in no spirits about the falls. I would not bring my mind to anything like eager expectation. I must have lost all my enthusiasm and am become dull and stupid. We went to Niagara Falls on the railway drawn by horses—therefore did not get quickly forward—but most of the long way was through wood or with nice cleared ground in view; there were some fine rocks with the river below us as calm as a lake, though the falls, to those who could hear, announced our near approach—and the spray was now visible. We stopped at a very large Inn at Niagara, with excellent rooms and fine airy passages, all handsome and comfortable; dined at 2, and then went to see this magnificent fall of waters. Anne was all eagerness and naturally, wishful to see all, but I was nervous and was not equal to going with her myself, nor could T.L. to those dizzy stations on the bank. It was rather hard on her to have her wishes and curiosity so much checked, but I could not see her go with only a stupid man (not a regular guide) to where a false step would have been destruction, at least it appeared so to me. Some other time she may have someone to take care of her, and have no nervous mother to prevent or check her adventurous spirit. She looked disappointed, but in the evening we took the falls from a different point, one superior in my opinion, and as we are to cross to the Canadian side tomorrow I trust she will feel much gratification without crossing planks! I shall only say that my first impression, I think, was something like disappointment—but the magnitude of water and its whole significance seems to grow upon you and you feel wonder, awe, and something still more as you contemplate it. I anticipated a roar of waters but the noise was by no means astounding nor any hindrance to conversation. We saw some Indians this evening for the first time. They had their blanket coats belted round them—wore hats and were well ornamented—their huts and homes are about 5 miles inland. They are a rich farming set, having land allotted them which they make productive, have a church and clergyman and are a civilized little community.

13th: Anne went out before breakfast to sketch—afterwards we crossed to the Canadian side in a rowing boat. It looked a little perilous from the eddying of the stream but we had passed over in 5 minutes without motion, but wet with the spray. We are at a large Hotel, with little company, immediately opposite the falls. After dinner we went to the Table Rock, a good station for seeing the falls—they are wonderful when you consider the immense body of water constantly falling. I do not consider it any advantage having the falls in full view from the Hotel: the spray too reaches the balcony, and the noise, though not deafening, is worrying. I think the rapids attract me more than the falls; I could have contemplated them for ever.

14th: An early breakfast as usual. My sister has had a disturbed night but was better after breakfast and we had one of the stages to ourselves to Queenston, where we were to take the Packet for Toronto. Dined there and embarked about 2: had a nice cool sail but nothing interesting, the land so far away, scarcely visible till we came in sight of the city, which appeared flat and agueish. Our road to the Hotel, on a wooden foot-path, with unpaved street, gave one at first a poor opinion of the Capital of Canada, and our reception at the Hotel was most uncomfortable, as we were shewn into a little, dirty, unbenched room, and the lodging-rooms offered us were up some stairs out of the yard. We objected to the accommodation and were afterwards promised better rooms when some company had vacated them, which would be in an hour. We were then shewn a very good sitting-room which we might have the use of, and given two very good double-bedded lodging-rooms, perhaps not the cleanest as in the States, but with which we were well satisfied. I fancy after our luggage arrived we appeared to the house better than at first they supposed us. Our apartments are in a private house adjoining and attached to the Hotel; it faces the lake, which is immediately across the street. Our terms as usual, taking our meals in the public rooms—the hours more like English—eight o'clock for breakfast, luncheon at one, and dinner at five. We are allowed tea in our private room.

15th: We took a carriage as we wished to see a little of the city and call upon one of our fellow-passengers in the *Independence.* The family have been out twenty-three years and have risen to very comfortable circumstances. They were fortunate in the purchase of a little strip of land about two miles from the town, on which, after it was cleared, they had built several detached houses, which appear quite in the country, in a nice quiet-looking lane, with the forest on one side and the houses and garden plots on the other. Their own little cottage is very pretty; the road is their private property and I can't fancy a nicer situation, the town being quite shut out.

The public table attendance is quite numerous and a Mr. Scott of the Athol family has his Indian wife with him—a modest timid-looking woman. They have been married only a few months. He has made immense purchases on Lake Huron far back, and is said to have a large fortune. Not having access to a Peerage we are in the mist as to his family; his younger brother is with him, looking more like an Indian than an Englishman. He is going to England to recover his patrimony.

The journal then relates how she was ill in Toronto and the party detained there in consequence for more than a fortnight.

August 4. Though I was still weak we embarked about ten o'clock in the evening in the steam packet for Port Hope. No sleep during the whole night; at 6 o'clock we disembarked and went to a disagreeable damp old inn for breakfast, and found that we had some hours to wait for the stages which were to convey us for about nine miles to Rice Lake, but we had a most agreeable specimen of Canadian hospitality from Captain Kingsmill.[1] He sent his carriage to convey the three ladies to his own house to await the time of setting out. We were introduced to his lady, a very nice woman, and we sat down to their family breakfast-table and received all the cheerful kind attention as if they had been old friends. T.L. had been introduced to the Captain at Toronto, who then offered his assistance to make any arrangement for us at Port Hope that would be of use in getting forward. The appearance of the village on the side of a hill, the houses interspersed among trees, had a most beautiful and striking effect when the sun rose—the fresh and lovely green of the foliage is different from anything I have seen in England, or it may be the clearness of the atmosphere that produces this effect to the eye.

The stage is a kind of wagon with two seats slung across, the back bound with buffalo-skin—and over good roads would not be an unpleasant carriage. Some part of the road was good, other parts very shaking and uneasy, but no corduroy. Captain Kingsmill told us he heard that John was waiting for us at Peterborough. We had two hours to wait for the steamer, which we tried to make less tedious by botanizing a little. The day was beautiful, not too hot yet bright. At last we saw a ponderous body slowly approaching us—it was certainly the most uncouth steam packet we had

[1] Probably Captain George Kingsmill, who had emigrated to Canada in 1829. He served as aide-de-camp to Sir Francis Head during the rebellion of 1837 and was High Constable of Toronto until 1846.

ever seen—it was the first on these lakes—its machinery of bad construction, and of slow motion. We dined on board, a comfortable clean dinner with few people. I was glad to get a sort of bed made up on a table with our pillows, bags, etc., for I began to be worn out. Whilst reposing the approach of a boat was announced and dear John was soon discovered as one of the rowers. He was soon on board and looked as much delighted to welcome us as we were to see him. With his naked brawny arms he scarcely looked like my once fair-skinned son, and his little Mambrino helmet of straw looked like nothing English, but it was John exactly in manner and looks, most happy. It was quite dark before reaching the place of disembarking, and we had then to be rowed up the river about a mile before reaching Peterborough: great alarm I believe felt for me but there were no serious bad effects. I was glad to go to bed, though with no very good prospects of a comfortable night: the room very small, never intended for family accommodation, three beds were all we could procure.

6th: Up in good time to meet John at breakfast: he and the young men who had come with him to row us were at another house—poor Anne not well, a sad drawback. In the course of the day we were introduced to the young men, and some ladies, John's acquaintances, called, I dare say all anxious to see what sort of people we were! There are some beautiful spots about Peterborough—a fine river, the Otonabee, with several small islands well wooded, which will retain their trees and render it very ornamental. The houses are numerous but yet seem to form no streets. They appear to be surrounded by the forest and the town has so different an appearance to anything we have been accustomed to that we cannot forget we are in Canada. The church stands on rising ground in the midst of trees. About it and that part of the town there are some sweet little openings. Anne in bed—but I was induced to take a walk in the evening to see some of the beauties: tired myself too much. We had several of the young men to tea, who, I fear, will be disappointed of their labours to-morrow, and John of bringing us up Sturgeon Lake in state, for Anne is in bed and very feverish this evening.

7th: We called in medical advice this morning. A very plain village-looking doctor attended, who gives us hopes it will pass off in a day or two, but recommends bed for to-day. The young men are all returning to their farms, and there is now such uncertainty of our motions that we shall engage our own boat, and John will receive us when we arrive. It is certainly a disappointment to us all, for Anne says John would have looked so proud and happy thus taking up his family. It is well to receive these checks sometimes.

We dine at the public table, with a small party of men, or perhaps gentlemen, living in Peterborough. We had again some friends of John's to call, one lady who was a Miss Hamilton[1], somewhat interesting to us. All the ladies seem to have a self-possessed manner as if accustomed to company. I had walked so much yesterday that I am not well today, and an anxious night about Anne perhaps increased my uncomfortable feelings nearly all day. I was never out, but there is no rest for the back on these wooden-bottomed chairs nor on the hard beds, all primitive. If one were quite well one might enjoy the variety.

8th: Anne is much better: a hot uncomfortable day with frequent showers. I went up the town with T.L. to our doctor's, did not however reach the house, went in to rest at one of these merchants' stores where everything appears for sale, but I fancy very dear. Very heavy rain came on with a little thunder: the evening very hot and close.

---

1 Major Hamilton, the father of this lady, had served in Egypt and elsewhere and on his retirement received a grant of land in Canada. He came to Peterborough in 1833 and purchased a grist mill and a saw mill by the Otonabee river. He had three sons and seven daughters and John Langton had become an intimate friend of the family. This friendship between the family and the Langtons was maintained, and there are many references to the members of the Hamilton family in these letters.

9th: It is a solace that we now the less regret not being up on Sturgeon Lake, as we should not have seen it to advantage on our first arrival.

10th: The weather is still so unsettled that we think it better to defer going, and now we cannot have the boat till Monday.

11th: Had more callers, the McDonalds, the member for the district, and Major Sharpe[1] and his lady: likewise the Duffies.

13th: We are watching with anxiety the weather and we are told this morning that it promises better; the party went to church. T.L. and Anne went to make calls. We had the Stewarts to call, who were I believe some of the first settlers in this part. Mrs. S.[2] a cousin of Miss Edgeworth's (perhaps not) is a remarkably nice woman, and her spirit and perseverance were the principal means of overcoming all difficulties. They have a family of ten children. Hamilton Dundas came to tea, a nice youth from Scotland coming out to settle, and recommended to Dennistoun,[3] who is a neighbour of John's. He interests me and I feel a sort of pity for him. Whilst we were sitting after tea our dear John entered, who has come with Need[4] and Atthill[5] to take us up to-

---

[1] This was Major Sharp, another retired military man who had settled at Peterborough. He is not mentioned again in these letters.

[2] Frances Stewart, wife of Thomas Alexander Stewart, emigrated to Canada in 1822. Extracts from her letters and journals were published after her death in 1872 under the title *Our Forest Home.*

[3] Robert Denistoun had taken up land on Cameron Lake a few years before. In 1839 he married one of Major Hamilton's daughters, as will be related later in these letters. He subsequently abandoned the Lakes, studied law, and became County Judge for the County of Peterborough.

[4] Thomas Need emigrated in 1832 and settled near the side of Bobcaygeon in 1833. After ten years he returned to England and died there some time after 1870. While still living in Canada he published his experiences under the title *Six Years in the Bush.*

[5] Richard Atthill was settled at the lower end of Sturgeon Lake. He subsequently gave up his farm and became a clergyman.

morrow, a most agreeable plan for us—I have dreaded the six miles on the waggon over hard roads as my head is very painful in moving about. It was decided I was not to attempt the wagon, but have Mrs. Fortye's[1] pony which was kindly offered.

14th: A promising morning, set off before eleven, I on horseback attended by Dundas. We unfortunately lost our way, which considerably lengthened the ride. John with the rest joined, and we proceeded to the boat stationed ready for us on Mud Lake. We were rowed by the three gentlemen and an assistant after the wind left us, and T.L. steered. I had a most comfortable bed made with pillows in the bow of the boat, thanks to dear John's care of me, so that I proceeded without fatigue. Some parts of the banks were rather pretty though generally flat. In about four hours we stopped at an Indian Station to eat our provisions: we had passed a considerable Indian village not long before—here was only one wigwam, and the inmates were all around a fire very much like our gipsy's with an awning of mats put up apparently for the old grandfather and the hounds. One woman was making a basket, the only one employed, the rest reclining on the grass. T.L. offered the old man some wine but he could not be induced to take it, nor his squaw nor the younger females. The remains of our provisions were received with pleasure. They seemed known to the young men, particularly to Need, who gave the old man an excellent character. We re-embarked, and in something more than two hours arrived at Bob Cajwin. The river before we reached it is very pretty, with more rock than we have seen before, and some rapids. A small log-house took in our luggage, and where the young men ordered dinner I was to sleep. We had to walk more than half a mile over a wretched unmade road quite in the wood to our sleeping-place, a nice clean log-house with a

1 Mrs. Fortye was a daughter of Major Hamilton whose husband managed the brewery and distillery in the ownership of which he was a partner of Major Hamilton.

nice clean hostess. We had a comfortable cup of tea and our beds look so clean that I shall be glad to lie down, but I do not feel worse for my day's journey, and highly gratified by John's affectionate care and kindness for his mother.

15th: The morning was wet and very unfavourable-looking; we were told that a fresh party of young men had arrived in the night and brought John's boat, the "Alice," and Wallis[1] with his. They had proceeded to the other tavern, but arrived soon after breakfast and we were introduced to Wallis, Dennistoun, Hamilton[2] and Savage. The colours on the boats looked gay and cheering and it soon began to clear and the sun to shine and we embarked. John placed the ladies on his boat and he and Hamilton rowed, Dundas steering. The scenery was flat, at Sturgeon Point interesting, where a collation had been prepared for us on the day we were first expected. The lake has little beauty or picturesque scenery, the banks are flat with no clearings on the left—a line of forest, but as we approached Blythe there were a few pretty inequalities in the banks, and about 6 o'clock we were rowed to the landing-place under a bright sun. Whilst disembarking the gents all seemed to disappear so that we found ourselves alone, and John led me up a most rugged path, seemingly very happy and proud to welcome his parents to his little habitation in the backwoods. All certainly looked wild, but his little cottage was made comfortable for our reception and promises snugness, but with primitive simplicity, where we may be very comfortable till our own house is ready to receive us. It is rather a pretty-looking cottage higher up from the lake. It looks naked, all the wood being cleared; but when a

[1] James Wallis became a life-long friend of the family. He came to Canada in 1832, but entered first into mercantile business in Montreal. After a visit to Fenelon Falls he entered into a partnership with Jameson and they built a saw-mill at the Falls. He also purchased land in the township. Wallis had a home at Fenelon Falls but after 1840 he moved to Peterborough. The mill continued to operate until 1858 when it was destroyed by fire.

[2] Gavin Hamilton, Major Hamilton's eldest son.

few plantations are made to ornament it, it will look very pretty. A happy comfortable tea postponed further examination of our new situation for this evening.

If God in his mercy grants us health we may be happy, free from many cares in this quiet retreat and may profit by it, waiting the next change with humble hopes of its being a blessed one.

I have brought this little journal to an end and have closed it.

Letter from Thomas Langton *to his son* William Langton *in Manchester, dated 20 July, 1837, from Toronto.*

I wrote to you from Niagara last, the moment we got to Manchester (for so the village on the American side of the Falls is called) but before we had made any attempt to get a near view. Neither observation nor description is my forte, and I shall therefore say little about them.

The following day, the 14th July, we arrived here, where we are likely to remain some time, for on our arrival, we found a letter from John informing us that from a variety of untoward circumstances he was much more backward with his building than he had reckoned on. His letter to New York had told us as much before, though without explaining the causes, which resolve themselves most into the lateness of the season. The elements, as he says, conspired against him. Indeed he must have been, and must still be, a good deal hurried, and his farming business will not have been the gainer by his extra occupations. I have informed him of our arrival, and that we shall not move until we hear from him again. A Montreal gentleman, formerly a Liverpool man, who had been at the Falls[1] to see Wallis and who had seen John, recognized and spoke to me on Tuesday (the eighteenth). John had not then got my letter. This gentleman thinks we might be accommodated till our house is ready at the Inn at the Falls, but we must wait for John's opinion.

[1] Fenelon Falls, known earlier as Cameron's Falls.

Postscript by ANNE LANGTON.

My father left this for a sketch, and I had certainly intended sending you my presumptuous representation of Niagara, but now I find the post is going off directly and I have barely time to add a few hurried lines. When people talk of being disappointed with the Falls I think they do not rightly understand their own feelings. I was (especially at first) unsatisfied, but it was not with them but with myself. I had a consciousness of the vastness of the scene and at the same time of my own incapacity to conceive it. I felt mortified by my ineffectual striving to grasp the idea in full. It takes some time to form any notion, and a much longer visit, I'm sure, than ours would be requisite to form an adequate conception of its grandeur and magnificence. Fancy what a person's idea of St. Peter's would be who had once been within its doors. So here as there you must ramble about and retrace your own steps many times before you can realize any just notion of the scale of magnificence before you. This is the great advantage of going onto the tower or to other situations where perhaps the views themselves may be partial or obscure, but they each and all assist in the expansion of one's imagination.

We were exceedingly pleased with the scenery on the Mohawk river along which the railway runs from Schenectady to Utica. It is mostly mild, with the exception of one very wild and magnificent Pass. Railroad speed is very inconvenient in a fine country.

The country through which the Erie Canal winds was to me far from uninteresting though chiefly very flat, but the dense forest and the new clearings, the stumps, the log houses, etc., etc., were all new and associated with all my anticipations for the future. For the first time I felt really like an emigrant making my progress towards the far West. On the banks of this lake as we coasted the American side from Rochester to Lewiston I almost sickened of the forest; never was anything so tame and uniform as its almost unbroken line. From the heights near Niagara you look over a plain as boundless as the ocean and entirely covered with forest. Here my conceptions of the *interminable* forest were greatly enlarged. The small portions of the northern shore of [Lake] Ontario which we have seen are a degree more interesting than its southern banks, but I believe our own neighbourhood is a good deal more so. I begin to long greatly to see this future home of ours. Meanwhile we are comfortable enough here, quiet in our own apartment, and getting reconciled to sitting down fifty or sixty every day. The queer people we sometimes see at the public table afford us conversation. We have one English gentleman with an Indian bride. He, we were first told, was the son of a nobleman, but I fancy that is a mistake, though he may be highly connected. Some say he is a son of Lord Henry Murray, but it must be a grandson because the name is not Murray but Scott. His squaw has no beauty to recommend her, and looks, poor thing, very uncomfortable.

Extract from a letter from THOMAS LANGTON *to his son* WILLIAM LANGTON *in Manchester, written from Toronto, probably about 10 August, 1837.*

I mentioned that John had not been able to make as good progress as he had originally calculated on. He does not, in a letter I have received, detail what the arrangements are which he has made for our accommodation, *as we shall soon meet,* but he tells me that he had first thought of putting us in the tavern at Fenelon Falls, but at last decided on the present plan (which he does not detail). On the false report that we were arrived at Port Hope, which is within 12 hours of Peterborough, he hastened down to the latter place to meet us, leaving everything at home at sixes and sevens, with Wallis presiding, putting up beds, and reducing things to order. He gives us also some advice as to our journey from here which will I trust be useful to us and enable us to get to Peterborough without much fatigue in about 18 hours, starting from here in the night steamer.

I saw Frank Bury yesterday for the first [time], his

steamer, the *Sir Robert Peel*, having only just got afloat and requiring, as he tells me, further alteration before she will go comfortably. She is as yet very crank and we shall therefore not take our passage with him, though he goes our way.

Another acquaintance we have made here is a medical man, who has come out for the last four years as the convoy superintendent of the emigrant pauper labourers whom Lord Egremont annually sends out. He has brought out 800 this year, who have been set down at Toronto principally, at Lord Egremont's expense. Lord Egremont and his committee who manage these matters for him have been desirous of providing also lands for these labourers and supporting them till they are able to pay for the land by their labour and their improvements. With these views the agent has been over and has surveyed a great deal of the country with assistant surveyors and guides, expecting to find the Governments here and at home disposed to facilitate his objects; but so far from it there would seem rather a disposition to discourage his plan, and a pretense of considering a sale of a large lot of land to him as a monopoly which they think ought not to be allowed, though very large lots have been sold, within the time Lord Egremont has been negotiating, at very low prices to people who were obviously and avowedly purchasing with the expectation of selling again at a profit. If the man had wanted to make a jobbing affair and had greased the right palm he might have had a fair chance of succeeding; but as for such philanthropical whims—they are mere bubbles I suppose in Sir Francis's estimation. From this gentleman who seems exceedingly well-informed on all such subjects I have got a great deal of information as to Canadian farming generally, but little that is very encouraging. He thinks that leaving out of the question the few lucky hits that have been made by shrewd men favoured by temporary fortunate circumstances, and the prizes that have been thrown into the hands of friends of Government, men in power and surveyors, who are paid for their trouble by lands and continue to get picked lots as their remuneration, leaving these out of the question, few or none can maintain themselves by mere farming, but that with a small income in addition to their farm they may live much more comfortably and respectably than they could at home with a larger income. This is meant of the gentleman farmer, but the labourer, who would have had difficulty in England in living without occasional assistance from the overseer, if sober and in good health never fails to do well. The fortunes that have been made have generally been by men who came without a shilling.

I have as yet said nothing of the trust we sometimes talked about. There is a great jarring of opinion here as to the expediency of suspending cash payments by the banks. If they are to continue to pay their notes and all claims in specie they can discount but little for commercial men, and all Sir Francis Head's popularity, where he was popular, hangs by a thread. He is for paying away, though those who can't move without discounts are thrown on their backs. In the Bank of Upper Canada the paying system prevails; they can in consequence discount little and from the new joint stock banks, starting just at the same moment, many of their good customers are expected to bolt, and it is thought that they cannot continue to pay the same dividends. They have of late paid ten percent. Mr. Ridout the banker did not talk to me of paying more than eight percent in future. This however would be great interest as the present premium of the shares is not more, I suppose, than three to five percent. The shares are fifty dollars or £12 10s of currency. If I can meet with seven or eight shares I should be disposed to take them; but in addition to the premium it was the Bank of Upper Canada that offered me an exchange of nine percent, when the Bank of British North America gave me eighteen percent and shares would probably have to be paid from notes of the Bank of Upper Canada or an agio given on others. Not that any of the banks have yet got the authority to suspend, but they wish for it, and the Bank of Upper Canada say they don't, which they stated as the ground for the poor exchange they offered me.

We shall embark on board the steamer on Friday evening about bed-time; at midnight she will put to sea, at six o'clock the following morning she will arrive at Port Hope where, by the friendly assistance of Captain Kingsmill to whom I have written, we expect to find conveyances ready to take us and our luggage on to Rice Lake in proper time to catch a steamer which will bring us to Peterborough before sunset. There John is to meet us with a crew of backwoodsmen, but whether he takes us up to Blythe in one or in two days my next must tell.

Extract from a letter from ANNE LANGTON *to* MRS. WILLIAM LANGTON, *22 August, 1837.*

During the week we remained at Peterborough the good people of the neighbourhood came dropping in upon us all the time, and others of them would have done so, but either thought we were gone before, or supposed we were staying longer, so that some of John's friends and acquaintances remain to be made known to us. At length, on Monday 14th, we set out for Blythe, John having arrived on the Sunday evening, accompanied by Need and Atthill, to convey us to our home. The party was increased by Mr. Dundas, a young Scotchman coming out to make a trial of the backwoods, and spend a couple of years with Dennistoun, whose cousin he is. We had made his acquaintance at Peterboro. The six miles to Mud Lake were performed in Mr. Shaw's "carriage," which is a wagon, having the reputation of a little spring in the benches, but how it gained it I cannot make out. My mother was mounted on a horse contributed by Mr. Fortye for our convenience, and well it was, for her head would never have stood the jolting of our vehicle. She began, however, by taking a much longer ride than there was any occasion for. She and Mr. Dundas contrived to lose their road, and, when it was discovered, John had a good run after them to bring them back. The scattered party, however, at length assembled and embarked with a fair wind on Mud Lake, to make the most of which a blanket and sheet were hoisted as sails. Do not suppose,

however, that the *Alice*[1] had such homely accoutrements.
We proceeded prosperously on our voyage, landing at Billy
M'Que's to refresh our crew, and give time for a storm
to blow over. His Indian family were all squatted on the
ground, in and about a little bark hut they live in in summer
in preference to their house, doing absolutely nothing, with
the exception of one old squaw who was weaving a basket.
In this state of complete idleness I believe they are always
to be found.

After contemplating this scene of laziness (I was going
to say wretchedness, but they looked happy) for about an
hour, and emptying the contents of our prog-basket, we re-
embarked and entered Bobcaygeon[2] River just as the evening closed in. I very much admired the scene, the wood
on either side is very beautiful. We landed at the foot of
the rapids, and walked about half a mile to our night's
quarters, where we were very comfortably accommodated,
though in a still more primitive way than at Peterboro.
This was at what was Mr. Sawers' house, which is now a
tavern. The young men all took up their quarters at the
old town at the foot of the rapids. About midnight there
was a rapping, and an enquiry made whether we had arrived.
Another party of backwoodsmen had come down to take
us up our own lake.

The following morning was most unpromising, and we
feared we were to have a complete wet day; but it cleared
up about twelve, and about two o'clock we set out on our
boat voyage, the ladies in the *Alice,* accompanied by John,
Mr. Hamilton and Mr. Dundas, my father in the *Calypso,*
a smaller boat belonging to Mr. Wallis, he, Dennistoun, and
Savage, being my father's companions. About six o'clock
the two boats reached the little landing-place at Blythe, and

---

[1] The *Alice* was a large boat with a sail, a gift from William to his
brother and brought up from Kingston. It was named after William
Langton's eldest daughter.
[2] The spelling varies in these letters according to the various attempts to reproduce the Indian name, but in this book the name
will be uniformly spelt as above.

we beheld our home. Our rowers all disappeared without waiting to receive our thanks, though I am sure they deserved them. Three times had some of them been down to Peterboro, some to Bobcaygeon, to meet us, to say nothing of a cold collation prepared for us on Sturgeon Point another day when we were expected and did not arrive. At last, however, after all delays and disappointments, our long journey is accomplished. John looked very proud when he handed his mother into his little mansion. His arrangements for our accommodation are very snug. Wallis has contributed a bed and some carpets. My mother and I sleep in the larger bedroom behind, Aunt Alice in the small one John used to occupy at first. My father has the hammock put up every night in the sitting-room, and John himself has a tiny apartment curtained off by a sail from the anteroom. Here we expect to make ourselves comfortable for perhaps a couple of months, or maybe more, if as many unexpected delays occur as have occurred in the preparations at "the big house" as our future habitation is elegantly denominated. But I suspect we shall summon the plasterer from "the big house" to stop up sundry chinks here which let in daylight now, and would admit quite too much of the winter blast for such delicate inmates as we are. And now you will ask what I think of the spot that has been so much talked of, and thought of, amongst us. Upon the whole very much what I expected to think of it. The picture my mind had formed of the Lake is really very correct; that of Blythe was so much more particular in all its details that it could not be quite so exact. What most strikes me is a greater degree of roughness in the farming, buildings, gardens, fences, and especially roads, than I had expected. But when one looks at the wild woods around, and thinks that from such a wilderness the present state of things has been brought out by a few hands, and how much there is for those few hands to be constantly doing, one's surprise vanishes, and one rather wonders that so much has been done, than that so much remains to be done. This certainly is a country where the virtue of patience will not languish for want of exercise. All around one sees such a multiplicity of things that should be done, and the ways and means to accomplish them so few and small. One can scarcely realise the difficulty there is in making away with the wood that encumbers the ground, except when a good burning is practicable, until one sees it lying. The stumps must give every place a rubbishy appearance, and the spreading roots prevent anything like a smooth pathway. Besides which stones are very abundant and a great obstacle to a neat garden. As a few years might make me forget the chief differences between here and England, I will tell you now, in case any of our friends should come out, that the paths and roads require that the supply of strong shoes should be good. Even in fine summer weather the frost will be wet, and you can never reckon upon going any distance without encountering some spot where the water has been dammed up by some wood obstruction. Most probably some more strong shoes will be my first commission. The opening to the lake is at present small, and we can only see from the house a small straight piece of the opposite bank, but this winter's chopping is to bring to view a pretty piece of land on our own side, and if the opening does not become too great there will be a decided improvement in the picturesque. Our house is a good deal above this, about a couple of hundred yards off. When you reach the summit of the hill, a short way behind, you look down into the main part of the clearing, and a pretty little valley it is. I have made no sketch of the place yet, but shall be on the lookout for a good point for one. At present I have been well occupied in looking about me within and without, penetrating the forest to the beaver meadow, or diving into the depths of the storeroom, where the traces of womankind may now be seen amongst the possessions of the bachelor. Occasionally I give half an hour to the garden, where at present the weeds are more abundant than the plants; but we are to blame in some measure for this, having come out from England earlier than advised by John, and the bustle of preparation for our house having thrown some minor matters behindhand. But I must resume the narrative of our proceedings. Our first day was spent in looking about John's premises, and making ourselves at home. On Thursday we went by invitation to see Fenelon Falls and dine with Mr. Wallis. My mother and Aunt Alice were neither of them well, and stayed to nurse each other. Mr Savage, who is a recent addition to the community, and not I suppose certainly a permanent one, came to help John row us up. The sail is pretty, the river as you approach the Falls very pretty.

The Falls themselves would be well represented by the sketch of the Canadian Fall at Niagara, except that the mill and its works would bear a very different proportion to the water to what any buildings about Niagara do, and, if coloured, the beautiful emerald green in the one must be a somewhat yellow line in the other. We walked about, and visited the new house of our entertainer, which is rather further advanced than our own. Its situation is extremely pretty, on a little plain, thinly scattered with trees, affording a natural lawn, and with very little trouble it will be a very pretty place. It is almost made to his hand. At dinner we had Captain Dobbs[1] and Mr. McLaren.[2] The latter, whose name will be new to you, fills a secondary situation in the increasing establishment at the Falls, superintending the commercial department there. After dinner I made a slight sketch of the church while the gentlemen took their second glasses of wine, and we then re-entered the *Alice* to return home. On our way we just missed the novel adventure of

---

[1] Captain Dobbs is only occasionally referred to in a letter to Thomas Langton dated January 9, 1834 (*Early Days in Upper Canada* pp. 51 et seq.). John Langton enumerates his neighbours on Sturgeon and Cameron Lakes and describes Captain Dobbs as follows: "An agreeable, gentlemanly, elderly man of whom I know nothing more than that he is reported to be an excellent chess player, and, what is of more importance, to be the father of six daughters." He seems to have occupied Jameson's house in his absence, and when the latter returned at the end of April, 1839, was dispossessed and left the neighbourhood.

[2] Mr. MacLaren was Mr. Wallis's partner and deputy in the management of the mills at Fenelon Falls. He was commonly known as the "Major," but had no military rank.

bringing down a buck in the water. We saw two swimming across the Lake, and followed both, the first, however, only with a view of seeing him land, but of the second we had a good chase, and were within three or four yards of him when he gained his feet. Had we perceived him a few seconds earlier we would have had success in the chase, and I should have taken some of the credit to myself, being on both occasions the one to perceive the branching horns of the game. It was about dark when we landed here. On Saturday John left us to go to Windsor[1] and give instructions about the sending up of our packages. I believe they are all arrived here in apparently good condition. The short journey they have still to perform presents more difficulties than all the rest, so we may yet have occasion for the philosophy we prepared ourselves with when we committed our property to the perils of so long a journey. We find also some difficulty in getting up a few things we were obliged to leave at Peterboro, the carrier who comes to Bobcaygeon three times a week promising to bring them up the next day, and they have not yet appeared. Where there is no competition people consult their own leisure and pleasure, and for these everybody must wait.

It was beautiful, and we had been dining as usual in the tent on Monday, when, a short time after we had quitted it, a sudden gust of wind tore it to the ground in a minute, and levelled some of the fences. If the storm has laid the mosquitoes and other insect plagues we shall rejoice, for we were annoyed by them. It is comforting to perceive that the residents of a longer standing suffer less, and when the land is pretty well cleared they apparently disappear. There were none at Peterboro, or at least very few. When the black fly makes its attacks you are kept on a perpetual smart all over the exposed parts, but I do not think they bite through thick leather as the mosquitoes do, neither are the effects quite so permanent.

[1] The old name of Whitby.

Extract from a letter from ANNE LANGTON, *September 1837.*

I am not a backwoodswoman yet in this, that I cannot feel easy when near the end of my stores. John thought my anxiety very laboured when I saw the bottom of my candle box. Here they have been so accustomed at times to be without things, that they take matters over and above easily. There is a very good store at the Falls, that is as good or better than any in Peterboro, but the difficulty of getting up goods makes the supply uncertain, and you are not to be surprised when told that the tea and rice are still on Lake Ontario, and that there are only three candles left. What should you think of a few pounds of tea coming at the bottom of a sack (without paper) and a few rusty nails at the other end of it? When I mention any of these primitive ways of doing things it is with the desire of making you more exactly conceive the precise style of civilization to which we have attained, not at all in the spirit of a grumbler, indeed it would be absurd to make grievances of such things; and after fastening your window with a string round a nail, or shading it with a boat flag for a month, you are very apt to forget that there is any other sort of hasp or blind. As I have not seen the interior of any backwoods establishment save this (for Wallis's being the tavern is not a specimen) I cannot give you much information. When we made our calls at Peterboro we were, with one exception, not received where the family were sitting. Painted wooden chairs are the most frequent, rush-bottomed ones being in the more elegant drawing-rooms. A papered room, save in the Government House, I have not seen since we entered the province. At the inn at Peterboro a looking-glass about the size of my hand, making my face as round as Alice's, used to depart from me every day, for the use of some other person, and then to re-appear. We used always to take our chairs with us to the dining-room. At our tea-table at Toronto a larger sized teapot acted the part of urn or kettle.

Not a drawer or cupboard is to be seen at any of the inns. To set against this, when we dined at the Falls at Wallis's, and I was shown upstairs to take off my bonnet, the toilet was neatly covered with white linen, and a little jug of warm water brought me with as much tidiness as in any house in England. As for provisions, bread, potatoes, and pork, with the produce of the dairy, are the unfailing ones, but they have been varied here by beef, venison, pigeon pies, and vegetables, of which there are, or may be, plenty in their seasons. There is very little in the way of fruit. John has some gooseberry and currant trees planted in his garden. These grow wild in the woods, and of the wild raspberry there is such plenty that they are sold at a shilling a pailful, gathered, I fancy, by the Indians. We were too late for these, and the cranberries, which are likewise plentiful, are not come in. At Toronto there was a miserable display of fruit in the market, and at the Government House, where there was every other luxury and elegance, one dish of the most wretched strawberries was the only fresh fruit they could give us in the middle of July.

Letter from MRS. LANGTON *to* WILLIAM LANGTON *dated 28 October, 1837.*

In our last despatch you had not one line from your mother, for the packet was unexpectedly called for and therefore, I being last on the writing list, it was obliged to go without my portion. I now mean to be the first in our monthly communication, for the former went by Mr. Need and if he was delayed in New York you will probably receive this before he presents himself with his budget of letters for you to distribute. He is in our opinion one of the most agreeable of the young men, though his appearance is less prepossessing than that of some of the others. He seems to be becoming a favourite even with the former grudgers.

We are still John's inmates in his shanty, for the kitchen is not yet finished off in a state to be used. Our furniture has now all arrived except the sofa and two other packages, one a chest of drawers, and the other a case of wine. The latter perhaps they keep back to partake thereof, for a box containing a dozen bottles of Geneva has been considerably robbed, two whole bottles taken and two or three half-emptied. Some wine has likewise been equally ill-treated. Our beds, about which I felt the most anxious, have arrived in really *good condition* considering the three trips John made in the scow to bring up the things from the Scugog River in most unfavourable weather. They were hard tugs for the rowers, and the packages were out likewise for the greatest part of the nights, but all appear, so far as they have been unpacked, in very fair condition and have suffered little damage, considering the change of conveyances and the slight packing of many articles. The chairs have escaped wonderfully. There is some little jingling in the box of glass, which makes me afraid that I cannot replace the egg-cups on John's table which now appear in place of tea-cups when there is an addition to the party. The bed-steads are now up in the rooms appropriated to their intended desti-nation. Our room is lined throughout with wood, and has a most comfortable appearance. Over the joining of the boards there is a moulding which is a pretty finish. Anne's room and my sister's will be hung with the material brought from Manchester, as well as the drawing-room. The dining-room, halls and staircase are to remain in their log state this winter, which does not give you the same naked cold, comfortless appearance as our plastered walls in England. These rooms are later to be lined with butternut which resembles walnut and grows here. The entrance and staircase are pretty, in a small way. Indeed there is nothing to wish different in the habitation except it be that the rooms had been higher and the third lodging-room somewhat larger. The yard and outhouses are not yet quite planned, and of course no preparation made for them this winter. No one can have any idea of the difficulty of getting anything done in the backwoods but those who have witnessed it. We may have thought John dilatory, but now we are surprised that he got anything done, workmen being so scarce and some of the work attended with great difficulty and requiring much labour, for instance the chimneys, and walling the well with stones, which were brought from the bottom of the lake, and then drawn up a steep and rugged rise, very hard work for both men and the poor animals. John has glazed the windows himself with the assistance of a day's work from one of his friends. No glazier is living in these parts, and for some time the contracting carpenter was the only man at work in the house, very slow work you must suppose. But in another week we hope to be set by our own fireside and busy making our little arrangements. Anne and John have been the only busy people in the cottage for the last week, the old ones remaining quiet, airing beds, etc. We have had a little smart frost and a covering of snow but it is now all gone, that is the snow, but the frost is coming again as it is now five degrees below the freezing point. We have had some beautiful weather, like the most beautiful of our days in April, perhaps something warmer. We have had one loss which made us look very serious at first, but we now find it will be of slight or indeed of no consequence. It was a loss of blankets, which must have been abstracted at Manchester from a wardrobe; the shelf containing (from our memorandum) several pairs was found empty, but sufficient remain in other drawers for every covering we shall want, and likewise for our servants when we get them, and we find that they now have blankets in the stores at Peterborough where John is going next week. Therefore do not fear that we shall suffer any want.

Mr. Wallis opened his new house a fortnight ago, and Mrs. Hamilton having some lady visitors from Peterborough John had the treat of some waltzing. (Anne declined joining the party.) The morning following the ladies came to call on us, attended by several of the young men in their blanket hunting coats with scarlet sashes and various furry caps. As they came up the path from the lake they made a gay and very interesting appearance, and likewise when they took their canoe to return. There are several very nice-looking young men, and perhaps you may be surprised when I say that John is about the handsomest of the set.

He is well bronzed, has got fine dark whiskers, and with his curling hair, sensible and animated countenance he will pass for good-looking anywhere, besides in the eye of his mother.

Wallis has been uncommonly kind in assisting John with a bed and little articles for our accommodation which his shanty did not afford. One was a carpet which is something the worse for our use of it, therefore we wish to give him the drugget we brought out for our drawing-room, as the Turkey carpet is the one we shall use this winter along with our old ones. Therefore by the first spring ship we shall want a little package sent out. But time enough for commissions when we find how the winter agrees with us, about which I stand in no little awe for some of the party. Could I maintain my present activity in moving about I should have no fears for myself in keeping up a tolerable degree of circulation and warmth with the aid of an effort of will. Our furs are all quite safe and in perfect preservation. They will soon be put in requisition, at least the hoods and boots. Our black velvet was a bad speculation, for the wood-ashes being white and very light we shall always look dusty, but *n'importe*.

God bless you all.

THOMAS LANGTON *continues the letter:*

October 29. Your mother seems hardly aware of the intensity of the frost, which this morning at half-past six o'clock was 21° out of doors, at seven it was 25° in Aunt Alice's room, who, notwithstanding she was an invalid, did not seem to have been inconvenienced by the cold. We have several times this month had a thermometer four or five degrees below the freezing point. On the 25th we had the first snow, which continued on the ground during the 26th, though it rained all day but froze as the rain reached the ground. To-day, notwithstanding the severity of the cold in the night and by day in the shade, the afternoon has been so delightful that Anne and I have taken a long walk in the clearing and in the woods. One cannot get over the ground so quickly as at Bryn Ganno and about Seedley, for one has to climb over fences and fallen trees, through closely grown underbrush, and, with a good deal of contrivance, to make good the crossing of creeks, which the late rains had swelled more than we had expected, but our walk has been very pleasant.

Your mother anticipates getting into the house in a week. I will give her two, and shall be glad to find us housed in that time. We have still some important outstanding inconveniences which will take John down again to Peterborough early in the week, and we have not yet engaged any servants though we have been making inquiries for some time. The abstraction of the blankets is an unpleasant circumstance, but considering that all the furniture had to be carried by hand from the Bank to Pickford's, that wardrobe tops are not susceptible of being locked from want of a bottom fastening, and that several of ours were left to be packed, that is matted etc., at Pickford's after we left town, it is well we have not been greater sufferers, and I am not aware that anything else appears to have been meddled with, though there is yet uncertainty.

As to my complaints—? I was not aware of any alteration in my looks—my spirits may not have been very good when in pain, but I have said little about it. The symptoms I consider no longer equivocal, and their rapid increase during the last month or two may well make one serious.[1]

We hope soon for better communications with the civilized world. After the New Year, Fenelon Falls will be a post-office town and henceforth your letters must be directed for us "Blythe, near Fenelon Falls, Upper Canada." The lock at Bobcaygeon is also nearly completed and there was a public meeting at Peterborough about a month ago for a steam-boat which was to ply between the Mud Lake, Pigeon Lake, Sturgeon Lake, the Scugog river (upon which a lock is also constructing) and Scugog Lake. At some not distant time the navigation is expected to be carried beyond Fenelon Falls (where three locks will be required) through Cameron

---

[1] He died six months later.

Lake and Balsam Lake to Lake Simcoe, and from thence to the northern part of Huron Lake and Lake Michigan. This looks rather like castle-building, but there is no doubt of the practicability of the thing, and when the works on the Trent river are completed comparatively little will remain to be done; and then, say the Peterborough people, we shall be an important commercial town. The expense of the steamboat is laid at £1500, which is to be raised by 120 shares at £12/10/-per share. About £1200 has been already subscribed. John has put himself down for two shares and me for the same. It will give a poor dividend at first, if any, but the advantage of having a regular communication with Peterborough will be well worth the interest of the money. The vessel is to be built at the Falls, the engine at Kingston, whither Wallis went last week to make arrangements. Wallis is Secretary and Treasurer, John is on the Committee.

I suppose the money market is again returned to its average state before the last convulsion, for John could only get nine percent premium for my last bill at Peterborough and was informed that the rate had fallen correspondingly at New York, Montreal and other places. Here we are very much in the dark about these matters. The Toronto papers which sometimes reach us do not quote exchanges, we see no New York papers, and our *Spectator* and *Albion* come so late and so irregularly that I think there must be unnecessary detention at some of the post-offices. Perhaps things will mend when we get a Post Office near us. I have heard the New York Post Office complained of, and if one had a friend there whom one was not afraid of troubling I should be for addressing all letters and papers to him with the understanding that he should forward them making a charge for his trouble. But it is not worth while.

Letter of 8 November, 1837 or earlier from ANNE *and* THOMAS LANGTON *to* WILLIAM LANGTON.

Though first on the sheet I am really the last writer, so had best be read last, for though a preface may very well be perused after a work an appendix would come very badly before one, and I suspect I have not much original matter for you but shall most probably write on the two engrossing subjects of my thoughts, the progress of the house, and of the season, with my hopes concerning the one and my fears respecting the other. I recollect when we took up our abode in our last habitation the board was spread there for the first time on the 15th of November and your and Margaret's health drunk in due form. Perhaps we may contrive to keep your wedding-day again in the like manner. We shall then have been exactly three months inhabitants of John's little mansion. I can scarcely believe I am not an older resident of the backwoods. The house promises to be very snug and comfortable in due time, and although it must remain short of some of its out-buildings this winter yet we shall find the possession of a kitchen a perfect luxury. The loss of John's was a very great one certainly,[1] but it appears to have been effectual in ridding us of the devourer more dreaded than mosquitoes. I shall send you a plan of our dwelling when we are settled, with the situation of all our pieces of furniture, that you may form something of a picture of our interior. I fancy this will probably be our last letter before the closing of the lake. How anxiously you will look for the one which will follow that event, which will tell you how our dear old people bear the cold. We shall at any rate take rather better care of ourselves than some of the older inhabitants. One of the ladies who came up the lakes a week or two ago, when there had been already sharp frosts, set out for this boating expedition of forty miles without a cloak and with open silk gloves. After the dinner at Wallis's new house and dancing till past midnight the party of ladies were rowed home between two and three miles. It had been freezing hard all day. Do you think my dear mother would ever trust her precious daughter to join in such a party? I am afraid when we envelop ourselves in our furs and flannels we shall appear ridiculous in the eyes of our neighbours,

[1] It was accidentally burnt down.

but I do not care much for that. I have great hopes we may acknowledge another letter from you before closing this. John is gone to the Falls and there was communication between that place and Peterboro' yesterday.

Extract from a letter from THOMAS LANGTON *to his son* WILLIAM, *"The New House, Blythe. 29 November, 1837."*

We were for a long time in alarm about servants. In three different journeys to Peterboro, and as many to Ops, it had been one of John's principal errands to engage a servant, or servants, and from each he returned unsuccessful.

I suppose there is the same reluctance to go so far back as we have found in Liverpool servants to engage far out of town. Whatever the cause may be, we could get no experienced servant from the more settled part of the country, and we had seen specimens of the new arrivals which were very discouraging. In these circumstances Anne, John, and I were, one Sunday afternoon about a month ago, going over the new house, and planning what was to be done, when a spare, decent-looking young man of the labouring class came upstairs to us, whom John greeted by the name of Dan. I immediately recollected the name as one of John's first acquaintances in the backwoods, and found it was actually Dan O'Flyn, who had come to repay John some money he had lent him last summer to enable him to procure some comforts for his old father and mother, who had come out to end their days with him.[1] John had great doubts about the eventual repayment, but the case was so parallel to his own

---

[1] John Langton made the acquaintance of Dan O'Flyn on his first visit to the Lakes in the autumn of 1833. He observed a disconsolate figure sitting by the Lake, who informed him that he had cleared his land two months before, and had come down to the Lake for the chance of seeing a fellow-creature. His land was two or three miles off. He at once took Langton under his special protection, assuming the position of mentor and *valet de chambre*, Langton in return taking charge of his money for him. Dan was very useful in assisting the process of bringing up the goods of the settlers who came from Peterboro together on that occasion, M'Andrew, Jameson, and Langton.

that he could not resist the appeal, and Dan now honourably redeemed his credit. He also applied for work, and in the course of the conversation it appeared that a daughter had accompanied the old folks, and though on enquiry we found she had never been in service, we proposed that she should return with Dan in the ensuing week, and be employed in scouring and washing out the rooms. The pair came to us about a week afterwards, and we found the sister a neat, cleanly, hard-working woman, who, though without experience as a servant, had been accustomed to have things comfortable at home. She is cheerful, disposed to be chatty without being too familiar, and without a spice of blarney. We have been all very much pleased with her, as you will judge from my having allowed her so much room in my letter. She has no objection to engage herself to us in any capacity, and left the wages to ourselves. I am only sorry she cannot be a permanent assistant. She is married, and her husband permitted her to accompany the old folks out, saying that if she gave him encouragement after having seen the country, he would follow. So that whether he comes out to her, or she returns to him, we cannot expect to retain the services of Mary Scarry beyond the ensuing summer.[1] In the meantime Mary makes us very comfortable, and we shall have time to look about us for a successor to her. We have a fine, cheerful, active lad of about sixteen, whose time is pretty fully taken up with cutting wood for the fires. The consumption of wood is awful. We burn, I think, on the average, about two trees *per diem*. A man goes into the bush, selects his trees, cuts down one, divests it of its branches and top, which are left there to rot. The oxen then drag it to the house, or woodyard. It is then chopped into lengths according to the several fire-places, and the lengths are split, except a few which are left whole for back logs. In a general way, I think two fifths of each tree is chopped into chips, a mountain of which accumulates about the yard, and is very diffi-

[1] Mary Scarry remained in Canada and was off and on the faithful servant at Blythe for many years, called in also on special occasions of trouble. She accompanied the family to Peterboro also in 1851.

cult to get rid of. When the clearing is extensive they have
to fetch the logs a good distance. One may say there is only
one sort of tree suitable for firewood, for there is always one
sort which burns better than the others, and as long as there
is a supply of that sort, no other will do. When that is exhausted the next best-burning wood will be the only sort.
As yet the sugar maple blazes away on every hearth. Its
destruction is of less consequence, as the maple sugar, if
made by hired labour, comes as dear as good Muscovado;
but the sugar-making takes place when the settler has little
to do, and if he has an active family they may supply themselves with sugar at a trifling expense. If they are not good
contrivers, or have burnt their maple trees, they must do
without.

Extract from a journal letter from ANNE LANGTON *to*
W. LANGTON, *11 December, 1837.*

Chopping is now about to commence, and in this I feel
very much interested, as a supply of firewood is of the utmost
importance. Hitherto the day's labour has supplied the consumption of the day, and when one sees what a heap of logs
disappear in a day, one can scarcely trust to the exertions of
one's chopper. It is rather a troublesome sort of fuel from
its bulk, its weight, and the rapidity with which it is consumed. Our logs (before chopping) are mostly three or four
feet long, and measure, at least some of them, as much in
circumference. The lodging-room fireplaces are of much
smaller dimensions but when a whole party have to be kept
warm you must have such a glow as shall oblige the circle
to be a wide one. The unsplit wood makes the most eco-
nomical fire, and a very warm one, though with a mixture of
the split it is more bright and cheerful. One large, sound
back log is, however, indispensable, and such a one we have
sometimes as takes two to carry it. You will think that my
thoughts run entirely upon heat and cold, but I can tell you
they have been in the glue-pot a great part of last week, or
buried in the contents of drawers and boxes. We do not
yet make very perceptible progress towards a settled state,

but I know we are advancing, though through very tangled paths. Meanwhile we are sufficiently comfortable to take things rather easily. Our sitting-room, though not yet adorned with its cotton hangings has all that is essential to comfort. I could very soon reconcile myself to its dark-looking log-walls, but the rough plaster between the logs is annoying. It is for ever crumbling down, and makes everything dusty. Our eyes have become a little familiarised with such things, and our room looks to me a very handsome one in spite of its rough barn-like appearance. The large Gothic window, however, improves the general look of the room. . . .

Baking is almost a daily operation, but not such a troublesome one in Mary's hands as it was with our former bakers. The usual plan in this country is to mix flour with warm salt and water, and set it by the fire to rise. But it must be carefully watched, the temperature must be kept even, no easy matter in cold weather. They usually put their vessel within another closed vessel of warm water, but even then it requires great attention, for if the fermentation is too long delayed it becomes sour. Moreover, whenever the right degree of fermentation is attained, then and there you must mix your loaf at whatever inconvenient season it may happen to occur. If the operation is successful you have very good bread, but there is great uncertainty in it. Our Mary's method is to boil hops in the water before mixing her rising, and to add a little maple sugar. This has the effect of making the rising keep a week or ten days, and there is not the necessity of the fermentation taking place soon. You may therefore bake several loaves in succession from the same rising, and the last will be as good as the first. In case of failure there is always a frying-pan cake to resort to, namely, unfermented dough baked in one cake about half an inch thick. I fancy it is bad taste, but I am very fond of these cakes, and were I keeping house for myself alone should occasionally have one as a variety. At present we bake in a bake-pan, but an oven is one of the things we intend to have next year.

December 15. Our thermometer has dropped below zero,

but the weather is calm and beautiful, and we contrive to keep the house very warm. In every way I have felt quite as cold in England as here, excepting that for ten minutes after my morning's toilet the tips of my fingers ache as they never did at home.

Extract from a letter from THOMAS LANGTON *to his son,* WILLIAM, *23 December, 1837.*

In this province the insurrection was suppressed and tranquillity restored before we heard of its interruption. How they are going on in Lower Canada you will hear almost as soon as we shall, for at this season our communications are very slow and limited. We have as yet only heard the first rather uncertain account of two villages being attacked, and I believe burnt, and probably the disturbances may not be subdued there so quickly as here, though from all I can hear there can be little doubt of the ultimate result being the same. Our invitations had gone forth to twelve gentlemen to dine with us on Christmas Day, when on the 19th a message was received from the Government by Wallis recommending the whole force of the townships of Fenelon and Verulam being called out to beset two roads into the Lower province —one about ten miles, the other about forty miles north of Fenelon Falls, by which it was thought Mackenzie might endeavour to escape. Dennistoun was therefore detached with twenty men to occupy these passes, where he would have had to bivouac in the woods with the thermometer at 12° below zero, and John was to have relieved him with twenty others on Monday the 25th for a week.

This put an end to our party, as we expected; but this morning intelligence was received that Mackenzie had succeeded in escaping into the States, so that there was an end to our soldiering for the present, and our party again revived with but short time for preparation.

1838

Account of the settlers in the townships of Fenelon and Verulam, 1838, by THOMAS LANGTON.

I begin at the North. The tailor *Allen,* who had given up his half lot and removed to Fenelon Falls, where he could take a town lot and follow his trade, has married a widow from the States. As they have no family I think he is wise to give up farming and stick to his business. His wife's younger son is our servant and a nice, handy, cheerful lad he is. We are well pleased with him.

William Jones is from the sister isle, where he is supposed to have left a wife behind. He might have sat to Captain Marryat for the character of Dick Short in Snarley-Yow, as far as regards taciturnity. He never speaks but when spoken to, and then in the fewest words possible, except indeed the Inniskillen Dragoons should come in question, when he is copious and eloquent. Not that he ever belonged to the corps, I should think, for he has nothing military in his bearing. He goes off to his own farm without notice, and comes back to work for John again without being asked. This might not suit with many, but he knows so well what is wanted, and is so steady at his work, objecting to nothing, however, that both parties seem suited.

Alexander Daniel is from Glasgow or thereabouts, former-ly a calico printer, then kept a shop, at which all his old fellow-workmen were customers, and had a thriving trade. "Why did you give it up, Daniel?" I asked. "Why," said he, after a pause, "it makes no matter telling any lies about it, I was too fond of my own whiskey." When he first came out he bought a "United Empire" right, and got it located in a different neighbourhood, but taking work with John, and preferring this situation, John made interest with the surveyor, and got his location changed. He appears very grateful to John. About a month after we got here his little boy came one day to beg a little whiskey and some sticking-plaster for his father, who had had his thumb nearly chopped off. John went immediately to him and found the thumb nearly severed at the joint, and hanging only by the skin and tendinous part under the thumb. The joint was not injured, except that a little cartilage was shaved off. John bound it up, secured it with splints and a bandage, and in ten days afterwards I found him chopping, and it has long been quite well again. He has had many severe mishaps, but is getting on well. He had sold his best milch cow to Jordan for twenty dollars, and the day before she was to have been delivered a tree he was chopping fell and killed her. Jordan agreed to take half the dead cow at the rate of the price he was to have given, though not half as much worth in beef as a milker. "But people are here very good to one another when any misfortune happens," said Daniel. He has recently had another mishap. One of his team of oxen had got into a neighbour's field, and was fired at with salt, as "breachy" cattle are sometimes dealt with. But either from forgetfulness or design the ram-rod was left in the barrel, and the poor ox was so injured that Daniel was obliged to kill him, and not only him but his companion, for oxen do not work well together unless brought up together. Daniel's spouse is a capital help-mate for a backwoodsman, for she can do the work of a man, as well as her own domestic duties.

William Jordan, the next to Daniel, is a very religious man. All his family attend prayers at John's whatever the weather may be. Understanding that he was going to kill a pig, and the family being very cleanly, I asked him to let me have some black puddings, but he told me he never made any, from conscientious motives, that it was unlawful to eat the blood, which was the life. I argued the matter with him in jest, and spoke of the superiority of a giblet pie, which contained a pudding of the blood, and he then rather inadvertently coincided with me, and said goose blood was the only kind he was fond of. Jordan drinks no spirits, not from conscientious, but from prudential motives, for he does not object to his children taking them occasionally. But he knows that if he begins it is not certain when he may stop, and that he is only safe by never taking any. The surveyor who came to run the lines, as mentioned before, slept at Jordan's, and speaking with me the following day he said he thought the Jordans were a very wordly-minded family, for that the girls were up before day-light, cleaning the house, making the fire, and preparing breakfast. The honourable gentleman is a Hibernian, and probably considers it best to take things easily in this world. Jordan's worldly-mindedness will, however, get him on well. He has a large, active, and industrious family, and is the most thriving amongst the neighbours.

Next comes *John Menzies,* who has bought half a United Empire lot from John, and has begun to clear it; but he is now engaged as John's regular servant, and lives in a house built for him on this farm. He is an intelligent and able man, and the most useful one John has yet had; but he has too good a place of it, I think, and has got the length of John's foot.

Ferguson Duke, or "Fergy" as he's called, is the last comer, a nice little and active man of whom I have a very good opinion.

The letters during the early months of 1838 were mainly concerned with the illness and death, on May 4, of Thomas Langton. He had many weeks of pain and suffering, borne with great patience and fortitude, before the end came.

Letter from JOHN LANGTON *to* HUGH HORNBY, *Liverpool, dated from Blythe, 20 February, 1838.*

I should have sooner written in answer to your kind

letter to my father to thank you and your brothers for your very handsome present, had I not wished at the same time to state in what I had employed it, and to show that I now so far see my way as to feel confident of being able to support myself in my present situation. The exchange was so high when my father arrived that we thought it best to draw immediately, but the banker to whom my father sold the Bill declined making any advances until he knew its fate. It was thus only the other day that I was able to appropriate the proceeds. One hundred pounds of this I have invested at 8 per cent and I hope to leave it untouched as a nucleus to which additions may be made from time to time. The remainder has been laid out principally in increasing my clearing, in additional buildings, etc. For the first two years after my arrival in this country everything was at a standstill, or rather retrograding, and as immigration was almost stopped we in the back country, whose sole dependence lay in an increasing population, suffered the most. After our first sanguine expectations had evaporated the prospect certainly was most dismal, and even when I came over to England, though I thought I saw symptoms of improvement, still I had my misgivings, and I must say that fears predominated over hopes, and had I been young enough to begin any new line of life I believe I should have left the country like many others. I am glad I did not, for though there is nothing very splendid to look forward to there is at any rate a certainty of being able to live decently, and when one has become attached to the life, as I am, and one sees few of one's friends better off than oneself, there is not much more to be wished. Everything in this world is by comparison, and you are no richer in England than I should be with £50 a year and my farm in Canada, that is in the backwoods. In the front, as we call it, i.e. in the older settled portions along the Great Lakes there are no doubt many men of substance, but they move in quite a different sphere from us, and by the time that our country is in the front it is to be hoped that we shall progress along with it. In the meantime we can live. My farm this year will yield about £40 profit besides paying my expenses of living, and this profit should annually increase. It is nearly double this year what it was last year, though the prices of produce are not nearly so high. At first the stumps, roots, and other encumbrances occupy about one quarter or one third of the surface, but these gradually disappear by cultivation, whilst the productiveness of the soil is in other ways increased—besides that the same buildings, stock and implements, etc., which I must have now would suffice for a farm nearly double the size of mine at present. These improvements certainly only proceed gradually, but when we have once got the footing we have now we may look to them with certainty. Even the war which seems impending over us cannot, I think, retard us much and it may do good. Upon the subject of this war allow me to say a few words which may not be useless, as you foreigners really seem to know very little about us. Almost the only English newspaper I see is the *Spectator,* a paper for which I used to have considerable respect. But though he commences most of his articles on Canada by lamenting the ignorance of the British nation concerning its colonies he seems to be fully as ignorant as the rest. To read him one would imagine that Sir Francis Head was a tyrant who, with all the officers of Government, the magistrates, and others in authority, had league with the Orangemen, and by the use of public money, intimidations and other illegal means had succeeded in turning the virtuous and enlightened Radicals out of Parliament at the last election. All this he learned from a certain Dr. Duncombe, and considering his ignorance of the man and his prejudices he may be excused for believing it. But when every one of the Doctor's facts have been refuted by the House of Assembly, not one of his own party attempting to defend them, when all the leading Radicals have disowned him and he was so ashamed of himself that for months he dared not take his seat in the House, surely the *Spectator* should have retracted. Even Joe Hume in a letter to the Doctor, lately seized amongst his papers, tells him in very intelligible language that he is a liar and a rascal. The real truth is that the

Radical party in this province is most insignificant, and had they not been bolstered up by the patronage of Hume and others at home, who I am convinced know as little of them as the nation at large, they would never have been heard of. There is no doubt a strong party of what are called Radicals at home, men who, justly perhaps complaining of one grievance, have other imaginary ones put into their heads; but those who call themselves Radicals here are in truth republicans, mostly Yankees, and they are both few in number and of little influence. These two parties coalesced in a great measure in the late parliament and were formidable, but when the true views of the Radicals became apparent, viz. shaking off the "baneful domination" as Hume called it, all men of whatever principles who wished to maintain the connexion with Great Britain united and gave the so-called Radicals a most signal defeat, caring little for the local politics of the candidate, provided he were a staunch constitutionalist. I am convinced that there are 99 constitutionalists to 1 Radical in the province. What your English prints make of our rebellion I do not know, but the fact is that Mackenzie had never 500 men in arms in the Home District and those were of the lowest rabble with few exceptions, and seemed more bent upon plunder than anything else. A few shots dispersed them and the projected rising in the London district never took place. And this would have ended this mighty rebellion but for the kind offices of our neighbours over the water. I am far from approving of the conduct of Sir Francis Head in allowing the insurgents to meet with arms and drill within four miles of the capital unmolested, but if he did allow it as a test of the loyalty of the province, as he asserts, certainly the result was most convincing. Not all the hopes even of plunder could draw 500 men to Mackenzie's standard, while almost every male inhabitant was in arms the moment the news of the insurrection reached them. Be it remembered that there was not one single soldier in the province. Unfortunately Mackenzie escaped to the States where he was supplied with arms, ammunition, provisions and recruits in abundance. Public meetings were held everywhere to further the cause of the patriots, as they were called, and whatever the Government of the States may say no one can doubt that they connived at least at these proceedings and at their seizing arms in the public arsenals. With this protection and assistance there were not 50 Canadians with Mackenzie on Navy Island. It was no longer rebellion but an invasion. Whether we were justified in burning the steamer *Caroline* may be a disputed point, but it undoubtedly brought matters to a crisis, and that and a similar seizure of a vessel at Detroit had the effect of making the Yankees vapour a good deal but checked their assistance to the rebels. Now everything appears quiet, though at the expense of several hundred thousand pounds. We have plenty of regular troops and more than plenty of embodied militia, and perfect reliance upon the loyalty of our own population. The House of Assembly pass very valiant resolutions and the Yankees in Congress make very valiant speeches, but in my opinion it will all blow over; at any rate it will depend entirely upon how old England takes it. I myself feel wonderfully indifferent about the great question of war or no war. As a man of peace, not endowed with any particular military ardour, I prefer the ploughshare to the sword. I should be considerably annoyed to have to march down to the frontier to be picked off by an American rifle, but at the same time I cannot shut my eyes to the fact that a war would pour a great number of British sovereigns into Canada and that the price of wheat would be much increased. Besides, when one fairly got warmed I do believe I should enjoy a shot at the Yankees. As yet the military mania has not reached us, though on the front everybody is mad. In the streets of Toronto every third man is a soldier, and at least every fifth an officer. Captains and colonels are as thick as blackberries, and the cavalry (lancers no less) are galloping about to the imminent risk of the lives of passers-by—and their own. Military tailors not being plentiful here, the variety in the uniforms is amusing and their cut as absurd as that of their wearers. But the article in greatest demand is a sword; anything with a hilt will sell for £5, if it also has a point it will fetch £10. If this humour holds, a cargo of scarlet cloth and gold lace would pay handsomely. Where the money comes from I know not; many a farm I fear will be changed into a uniform. One advantage of a war will be that the money of fools will migrate into the pockets of the wise. There is some advantage in living in the wilderness; the news of the insurrection never reached us until ten days after all was over, though it took place less than 100 miles off, so we were saved a march to Toronto to show our loyalty. We have to boast of one military exploit however. Whilst Mackenzie was escaping to the States it was reported that he had been seen in one of the back townships in the disguise of an Indian, and we in consequence received an order to send a party to guard a chain of waters used by the Indians in going from our lakes to the Ottawa, situated about 30 miles back of us and 25 beyond the last habitation, by which pass it was thought he might attempt to reach the lower province. My neighbour Dennistoun, a cousin of the stammering gentleman of that name whom you know, volunteered to take the command, and I was to relieve him in a week. As good luck would have it we got news of Mackenzie's escape the night before I was to have started, and I was not sorry to miss a walk through the bush of that distance, with eight days' provisions on my back, not to mention sleeping out on the snow in December.

Extract from a letter from ANNE LANGTON *dated 19 May, 1838.*

We had the "burn" a few days ago, rather an exciting proceeding, and at times exceedingly picturesque and beautiful. There was nothing to prevent our giving due admiration to the grandeur of the destructive element; it was accomplishing nothing but good. The brush heaps are immense piles, and blaze up furiously. There was a little wind in a favourable direction, which carried the smoke into the wood, where it mingled with the trees very beautifully.

The main part of the conflagration was over before night, but the scene was very pretty when the darkness came on, reminding us of an illuminated amphitheatre. Unfortunately a thunder-storm with much heavy rain came on the next morning, or the consuming of the encumbrance of the ground would have gone on for a week or more. . . . I am struck with the variableness of our climate during the spring and autumn months. I think the changes are quite as frequent and quite as great as in England, but the clear and fine weather prevails more here than with you. Now, however, on the 19th of May, there is never a leaf except on John's gooseberry bush, which is just beginning to show some green. We have got, however, some very ornamental wild flowers in boxes in our drawing-room window. My mother's garden will not make much way this year, owing to the amount of rubbish yet about the place. John has made his very nice and neat this spring.

During the first years of the settlement of the family on Sturgeon Lake it was necessary to send them supplies from England. Their safe arrival was a source of great anxiety at Blythe. Sometimes, owing to the state of the lakes or the roads, their transmission from Cobourg or Peterborough was considerably delayed. In connection with these packages, as well as other goods, there are frequent allusions to "Purdy's," now the town of Lindsay. Purdy had built a mill on the Scugog River, with a very large mill dam. He had also a store-house, in which packages were kept until they could be conveyed further north.

From the journal of Anne Langton *for October, 1838.*

Did you ever write a journal with the intention of sending it to any one? I think it would be difficult to do it with simplicity. . . . I made a commencement in the summer, but circumstances soon interrupted me, and I am sorry that I have lost the two or three days' record, for I think it was rather characteristic of the backwoods, and amongst other singular employments presented my mother manufacturing putty, and myself glazing windows.

Saturday, October 6. Got all the mosquito curtains and blinds stowed away. A change of weather, thunder and lightning, some heavy rain with promise of more, which will be good for the conflagration in the woods on both sides of us. The woods on one side took fire from the ashes of John Menzies' pipe, and all being very dry, and the wind very high, we were in some alarm lest Dr. Diehl's[1] trees should be killed and spoil our view. On the other side the fires spread across the creek from the burning log heaps and were still spreading and threatening our store of firewood when I visited them. John glazed a few panes, but the putty does not hold out.

Sunday, October 7. It is more inclined to freeze than on any day we have had this year. I begin to think a little more about frost and snow than I have done this long time, and wonder how I shall like them on second trial. The transition from summer to winter will, I expect, be rather sudden. Last fall we had very sharp frosts before this time. This year we seem quite to have had a second summer since the flies left us, but it has been an uncommon one. John says he has seen ice in every month in the year excepting July, and he is not quite sure about that month, but certainly as late as June 29, and again at the very beginning of August. I have had a cold, the first since I came to this country, not a bad one; but the spell is broken, and I am sorry for it.

Wednesday, October 10. Again an uninteresting day, but rather a busy one. It is our wash, and though John is away, we are not a small family, the party in the kitchen being ten this day or two. Six or seven are at present our usual number. We certainly have been rather a bustling family this summer, and when I look back I sometimes wonder how we managed for those months when we had no fire in the house, and every culinary operation, from baking bread to heating water, was performed on a dilapidated cooking

[1] The lot on the lake next to John Langton's farm was owned by a Dr. Diehl, who never made his appearance and eventually sold it.

stove, whilst eight or nine meals were regularly served each day and ten or twelve mouths fed with bread. This stove stands about ten yards from the back door, under a little shed. It measures 2 feet 7 inches each way. The chimney pipe rises at the top, an oval kettle fits into one side, a deep pan with a steamer above it into the other side, and a large boiler on a bake-pan at the bottom, each hole having an iron lid, when the vessels are not in, on which you may then place smaller saucepans, or heat irons, etc. The front of the stove has an upper and lower door and a little hearth—formerly there was something of an oven within, but it was out of repair before I was acquainted with it, now there is only an iron plate, which enables you to have your fire on the upper or lower storey. Here was many a nice dinner cooked with all proper varieties for a party of five or six (sometimes more), besides the eternal almost daily bread-baking, and everlasting frying for breakfasts and suppers. We have now had an oven built, and a great relief it is, besides setting the bake-pans at liberty, whose perpetual occupation was a great inconvenience. We have made many experiments in the bread-baking way. I think I told you we patronised hop-rising, but some failures led us to try the common salt-rising, and the votes were in favour of it. At one time we baked a great deal of leaven bread, but though frequently very successful, we also often had a sour loaf; now the president of the cooking department gives us hop-rising bread, and I am inclined to hope we shall be more faithful to it than before. Our wash-house has lately become serviceable, and so by degrees we are getting forward, and in due time shall have things complete and comfortable, and wonder how so many conveniences could be dispensed with. Very little can be done this year in the way of smoothing, or levelling; what is some time to be a lawn and garden is all still in the rough, and I daresay we must exercise our patience some time longer.

Thursday, October 11. A cold raw day. After a few household occupations, I was attacking in good earnest a job in the upholstering line, which had been hanging on hand for some time, when I was first agreeably interrupted by letters from England, and afterwards by one from John, saying he had to attend the Quarter Sessions, and could not tell when he should be at home. I was sufficiently disappointed just to ask myself the question how I should like a three or four months' absence. John's despatch was brought by a plasterer, obtained from Peterboro, and now we are really going to have the rooms underdrawn. Of course the house will be turned upside down for a time, and maybe my letter, along with other things, may be laid aside; but when I resume it I shall have to tell you that we have got a very good job done. You cannot imagine how perfectly *comme il faut* rough log walls appear to us now; when we have got our striped green print up we shall feel as grand as Queen Victoria amidst the damask hangings at Buckingham Palace. Hitherto I fancy we have more English elegancies about us than most of our neighbours, but the Dunsfords, I expect, will quite eclipse us, for they, it is said, are bringing a carriage out with them. I hope they do not forget to bring a good road too.

Saturday, October 13. We had a sharp frost last night, the thermometer was still some degrees below the freezing point when I looked at it this morning, and there was thick ice; nevertheless we have felt less cold than yesterday. It is my comfort when sadly starved to think that this coming season of the year has always appeared to me the worst; when once there is no possibility of being too warm, then there is a chance of being warm enough. I was busy with my bed-hangings again this morning, and since dinner have been doing another sketch for you. I think in time you will have some sort of a notion what this world of ours is like. We had once planned this autumn to go down to Bobcaygeon, stay a night there, and get some sketches of the town and of the lake, but it is now quite clear that we must wait for another season, for which I consider the regatta to blame. How all the bustle of that week seems to have faded from one's mind! I could fancy it was at least six months since the flags were fluttering, the sails swelling, the oars splashing, and the water sparkling, about Sturgeon Point, and that woody promontory itself covered with beauty and fashion, as the phrase is. Before it we had been more than nine months without seeing a single lady, excepting that once, through the telescope, I spied Mrs. Hamilton in a boat. I am sometimes reminded of my early years and companionship with boys only; perhaps you would think my feminine manners in danger if you were to see me steering a boat for my gentleman rowers, or maybe handling the ropes a little in sailing, but don't be alarmed; though such things do occur occasionally, they are rather infrequent, and my woman's avocations will always, I think, more than counterbalance them. I said I was often reminded of my early years. I have caught myself wishing an old long-forgotten wish that I had been born of the rougher sex. Women are very dependent here, and give a great deal of trouble; we feel our weakness more than anywhere else. This, I cannot but think, has a slight tendency to sink us, it may be, into a more natural and proper sphere than the one we occupy in over-civilized life, as the thing I mean and feel, though I do not express it well, operates, I believe, as a safeguard to our feminine virtues, such virtues. I mean, as the Apostles recommended to us, for I think here a woman must be respectable to meet with consideration and respect. The greatest danger, I think, we all run from our peculiar mode of life is that of becoming selfish and narrow-minded. We live so much to ourselves and mix so exclusively with one community. It is not only that the individuals are few, but the degrees and classes we come in contact with are still more limited. Those who have come to this country before their thinking and feeling years ought, I think, all to go back to the old world for a time, just to look above and below them; and how many new emotions they would have to experience! Here we know that the world is wide, but we do not feel its wideness. A long meditation sometimes on the former chapters of my life brings me down to something more like my real proportions, but self and self's concerns expand very rapidly when the pressure of the past is removed. We certainly do not gain many new ideas, and must consequently fall a little behind our age. My knowledge, even of the country I live in, increases very slowly since my dear father's intelligent and comprehensive questionings have ceased to elicit information.

Monday, October 15. We had a mild, hazy day—very pleasant after the frost. Our Sunday congregation assembled in the kitchen, which was so hot that we were obliged to set open the back door, notwithstanding the occasional intrusion of dogs, cats and poultry. We had a bride and bridegroom at church, Jordan's eldest daughter, who was married a week or two ago. The young man has land near her father, so we have another settled family in the neighbourhood. One of our new pair of blankets went as a wedding present to the young couple, for we feel ourselves now so well stocked as to be able to spare them. We shall never get into the way, I think, of heaping as many blankets upon us as people do here. One warm night in June Mr. Dennistoun, finding himself a little too hot, began to take off some of his coverings, and found he had been sleeping under eight blankets. This morning was beautiful; it was just freezing but no more, and there was a fog over the lake. These lake fogs are sometimes exceedingly picturesque, rolling up or down the lake with the wind.

The morning was devoted to clearing out the cellars, and stowing away their various contents, wherever there was room, and now the hammering is removed below-stairs. In the afternoon I took a solitary walk to the wood, and skirted it for some time, in search of a point from which the house might look well in a sketch. I cannot quite please myself, but I think I shall try another representation of it some day. I left the beaten track altogether, and shall pay the penalty to-night by a long darn. It is just a week since I visited the woods before, and a great change it has made. They are getting very thin and the ground is well carpeted with red and yellow leaves. . . .

When John returned from his trip to the "Front" last

night, we very soon got upon the subject of matrimony, a very favourite topic with him at present; but though much in his head, I do not think it has reached his heart yet. I wish he may meet with a wife for his own sake most sincerely, though I think it very questionable whether it would not be for my happiness that he should continue to want his sister. There is so much happiness, under every disadvantage, in having an object in life, and feeling yourself of real use to some one, that I think even selfishness would induce me to remain with him, whilst unmarried, unless, indeed, I should happen to marry myself, which thing was never less likely. I will here thank you for the kind wish expressed that, in the event of my returning to England, I should make your house my home. I am perfectly convinced of your endeavour to make it a happy one to me should I do so, and I think I may trust to your kindness still further, and believe that you would not attribute it to any want of grateful and sisterly affection if I should not do so. But the morrow must take thought for the things of itself.

One of the novelties John saw on his late trip was a lady knitting a pair of stockings in one, that is, doing double knitting from top to toe, and after taking off the latter, having the one stocking completed within the other. This will be more interesting to Cicely than to you. The lady thought it saved time, I cannot understand how it should do so. I do not, however, comprehend the performance exactly; perhaps I may be able to obtain some further information through John. I am now knitting him a pair of mitts for driving in, having a forefinger as well as thumb distinct, with space, however, for it to join its three companions, when not requiring its own separate home.

Tuesday, October 16. I put the finishing stroke really to my bed-hangings this morning, and no sooner had done so, than we determined to attack the dining-room curtains, for the plasterer has completed his work there and we are in hopes of getting the room finished off before Saturday, when John entertains the gentlemen of the Verulam and Fenelon

Hunt. He is to have his dinner at his own house, and
adjourn here to tea. This is the third time that such a party
has been planned, and bad weather, or something or other,
has prevented it from taking place. I hope this will go on,
and also go off, well. John got back from the Falls this
morning; he had not been able to get his load before dark
last night. I had been flattering myself that we were pretty
comfortably settled with servants, and therefore am much
disappointed to find we have another change in prospect.
Our housemaid informs us that she never stays from home
in the winter, and that she never intended remaining more
than three months. Of this we were never informed, or we
certainly should not have engaged her. This, I suppose, is
one of the troubles of the backwoods; there is so much expense
and loss of time in hunting for a servant here that it is doubly
annoying. However, it is not such a calamity to be left without
as it would be at home. Last winter we spared our only woman
twice, once for a week and again for a fortnight, on the
latter occasion having company in the house. Mr. Savage
was staying for the sugar-making with us, indeed he had
come into the kitchen and helped me to set a pan upon the
fire. How strangely one's ideas accommodate themselves to
the ways and necessities of the country one is in! This
summer, when our bustling household made a little help
from the ladies often necessary, I used to be amused at
myself going so composedly about my duties at the cooking-
stove, in full sight of Mr. Atthill, occupied in the joiner's
shop. One would feel shocked at such observation in
England.

Wednesday, October 17. This morning my mother and I
cut up a little porkling we had killed yesterday, and we
agreed, when on a small scale, it was more agreeable to operate ourselves than stand by and give directions.

Thursday, October 18. . . . Our confusion increases, and
will increase still more, though we shall have a habitable
room below-stairs after this week; yet lath and plaster will
be about all the next one, and I fear longer. We have

finished the dining-room curtains to-day; I should be sorry to do such stiff sewing in the depth of winter, from what I recollect of my finger-ends last year in hard frost. My hands are not given to chap much, but just the end of my thumb and forefinger used to crack, and get deeper and deeper for two or three weeks. It is surprising how much annoyance so small a thing can give. I am afraid I shall be softer about cold this year than I was last year. Then anything short of freezing to death was an agreeable surprise; of course you understand the expression in a modified sense. John says he minds the winter much more than he used to do; after all it is the length of it, rather than its severity, which is so very appalling.

Friday, October 19. I have no variety for you to-day, nothing but confusion throughout; the smoke, too, conspired against us, and turned us out of our principal upstairs sitting-room. We are now all congregated together in Aunt Alice's room. It is not often that the wind comes from this quarter. I only saw our room once or twice during last winter in the state it was this morning. It has been a more thoroughly rainy day than we have seen for some time, and promises ill for John's party to-morrow. We got the dining-room put in order again to-day. Whilst the workmen were at dinner my mother possessed herself of the plasterer's trowel, and proved that she understood the trade by performing a neat repair about the dining-room fireplace. A hearth here can never look as neat as at home; there is not half the satisfaction in sweeping up that there is when there is a grate to sweep under; but if I should sometime again have the pleasure of putting the poker into a good coal fire, scaling the bottom bar and brushing up, I have no doubt I should find myself longing for a glowing pile of Canadian maple. I have a remembrance, too, of a black-looking fire and a housemaid's long face as she said that it would not kindle for the chips were done, an unheard of calamity in this country; they accumulate only too fast, when the chopping goes forward. I have not visited the fires in the woods lately, for though I believe they are not even yet extinguished, the

weather has been such that they certainly cannot have
spread. The woods are changing very rapidly; I expect a few
more days will clear them of all their leaves. I am afraid
my journal becomes very stupid; it is rather unfortunate that
you should come in for all the plastering, it is somewhat
stupefying. I expect, however, we shall have much comfort
from our present derangement when it is all over; our rooms
will be warmer, although the sun will not shine so brightly
through the walls as it used to do, and we shall not need to
go round stuffing with cotton wool, and pasting brown paper
over the holes as we did last winter. Moreover, every word
spoken above-stairs will not be heard below-stairs, and *vice
versa,* neither will it be necessary, when washing an upper
room, to cover all the furniture in the room below it, etc.
Though our floors appeared very well laid in the first place,
yet the shrinking of the wood made many a wide gap in
them. There is no such thing as getting seasoned wood for
building, and scarcely such a thing as making full allowance
for shrinking in cases where you may attempt to make it, so
that for a length of time many a little alteration or re-adjust-
ment is becoming necessary.

Sunday, October 21. Yesterday was again a wet day, but
not so wet as Friday, for I made a great many journeys
down to John's and only came in for one shower; yet the
weather was so unfavourable that John felt quite certain
none of his party would come. Our preparations, however,
of course went on, and as we had a nice dinner ready for
them I was well pleased, just before dark, to see a boat
making its way to the landing. The guests were five out of
the eight who were to have assembled, the defaulters being
the gentlemen from the lower end of the lake, on account of
the weather, and Mr. Wallis, through indisposition. Those
present were Mr. M'Laren (Mr. W.'s right hand), Captain
Dobbs, Mr. Hamilton, Mr. Dennistoun, and Mr. Dundas.
Perhaps you would like to know what we gave them for
dinner. Soup, boiled pork (the national dish), stewed goose,
and chicken pie, with vegetables. Second course—plum

pudding, apple-tart, and a trifle. These all had to be carried down a slippery hill on a dark night, but everything, I understand, arrived safe, and full justice was done to our cookery. Between nine and ten our receiving-room began to fill with blanket coats, and I assure you when such is the costume, a room fills much faster than at any other time. We had tea and a very chatty evening, all being in good spirits, except poor Captain Dobbs, who is just about to leave the neighbourhood for the winter. The old man is sadly quizzed by the younger ones. He doubtless lays himself open to it, but I wish they would have a little more mercy. Our room looked exceedingly snug and English, with its Turkey carpet, its crimson curtains, and its ceiling, even notwithstanding its log walls. Mr. Atthill, I understand, is ordained, and will be in these parts again before long. He will, I hope, make a useful minister in our poor neglected country. The Dunsford family has arrived, not on the lake, but somewhere in this country, on their road towards it. Five young ladies all grown up! What a commotion they may make amongst us! This morning the same party assembled to tea, coffee, and water porridge—a great favourite with most of the backwoodsmen. They departed before our congregation met. We had an excellent sermon on evil-speaking, and by way of showing how much we had profited by it, we began talking over the weak points of our several neighbours immediately afterwards.

Aunt Alice is looking very melancholy to-night, her watch refuses to go, the clock stopped yesterday, my watch is gone to England, my mother's to Peterboro, there is a general strike among the time-showers. Fortunately my mother has a second old watch, on which we all now depend. . . .

Thursday, October 25. . . . This morning I took a walk through the bush, for the purpose of calling in Mrs. Daniel's assistance for a grand scrubbing day tomorrow. She promises to come, though she seems a little overwhelmed with business herself, as they had killed an ox a day or two before, and she had had to assist her husband in flaying, cutting up, etc.; and when the butcher's part is over, I know well from our own experience how much labour there is in turning head, heels, tallow, etc., all to the best account. The shanty showed evidence of the work that had been going forward. In coming back I visited a new house that Jordan has been building, the only edifice of squared logs besides our own that there is about. I then called in to see Mrs. Jordan, and compliment her on her new mansion. Nearer to ourselves I found another house, sprung up since I had been on the road, of which I had never heard a word. It is Allen's. He and his three step-sons, of whom our William is one, were busy working at it, and this family will be one of our near neighbours in about a week. If they chop with judgment this winter I think the new building will afford me a pretty sketch in spring. I made one more call on my way home, on Mrs. Ferguson Duke, and then I thought I had transacted a great deal of business, just as you might have done after spending a morning with your card-case in hand. Oh! there are exemptions and privileges in the backwoods. The last expedition I had made so far was on a beautiful July evening, when Mrs. Daniel's baby had been taken very ill in convulsions, and I set out with my mother's instructions and prescriptions, attended by one of our maidens, just at sunset. Our homeward path was illuminated by a beautiful moon, fireflies, and phosphoric wood. This was the first and also the last time I have seen the eternal forest under Luna's dominion. The little sufferer of that day is now a fine healthy child. We have had rain again, and the lake rises so fast that I am afraid my newly discovered promenade will be soon under water. It has certainly been very fortunate for our plasterer's operations that the frost has kept off so long. He is now going to plaster Mr. Wallis' house and the church. I am truly sorry for Mr. Wallis, having all to come that we have just gone through. I have been making experiments to-day in my room, to see whether there be no possibility of warming it this winter, and I am happy to say, after dismissing one stove, and putting up another, that I see a good prospect of this addition to our comfort. However, I feel half blinded to-night from the smoke I have been in most of the afternoon.

Sunday, October 28. I think you will not be surprised that the business of Friday and Saturday afforded me nothing interesting to relate. Peace and quietness is at last restored, and order also everywhere but in the drawing-room, which we may not perhaps refit in a hurry, especially if we determine to hang it at once. I think it very probable we shall live a good deal in one room this winter for the sake of warmth, and the Turkey carpet will be very likely to make the choice fall upon the dining-room; there are double windows, however, to throw into the other side. We have been sadly thrown back in our proceedings by the loss of the putty, which John had provided at Peterboro, and sent up by the boat, whilst he went down to the front. The glass arrived safe, but the putty was lost on the way, and there is none, nor materials for making it, in these parts at present, so that our new building must continue to admit the winter cold in every room. Perhaps some one similarly situated possessed themselves of it. There is a sad scrambling for some of the necessaries of life sometimes. There was only one box of soap to be had in Peterboro, which John and Mr. Dennistoun obtained, and were to have divided, but, coming up unattended, it was intercepted, and parcelled out at Bobcaygeon. Luckily John had been able to procure another at Cobourg, but neither that place nor Peterboro could furnish any candles; lamp oil is also not to be obtained at present. I hope there will be an arrival of some of these necessities before the frost, though our English supplies make us in some measure independent. We are talking of making soap; hitherto we have not done so, having only one servant and few conveniences. . . . I should tell you that both the clock and Aunt Alice's watch have taken to going again, and to counterbalance this good news, I must say I have no hope that my room can retain its warming apparatus.

Monday, October 29. . . . My mother and aunt I left very busy melting lead to solder a broken candlestick, and evidently enjoying an occupation associated with many youthful reminiscences.

Tuesday, October 30. A fine frosty morning led me to set out early in the day for another walk on the margin of the lake, bent upon exploring the coast a little further whilst the state of the waters admits of it. . . . On my way I stumbled upon a deserted Indian encampment, where the business of canoe-making had been going on with great activity. A little further I was rather surprised to meet a man, but I have no doubt the man was much more surprised to meet a woman. When I got home I found my two hours' absence had alarmed my mother; she had sent John in search of me, supposing I had either stuck fast in a swamp, or got fairly bewildered in the woods. I have not the character of being half as prudent as I really am. I am aware of the liability there is of getting entangled in the forest if you venture far, and am very cautious. I think I must have taken some of these walks in order to have my adventures to relate, for I do not suppose during the preceding year I have made so many expeditions as I have this month. There is only one more day left of it, and I think I must then bring my journal to a close for the present. I have enjoyed writing it very much, and I shall have great pleasure in sending you another month some other time.

The last of the month, October 31, is indeed most different from the first, the thermometer down at eleven with a sharp wind. We were, however, too busy to think about cold. Both an ox and a pig died the day before. I need say no more—give the reins to your imagination to fill up the details of our morning. Before dinner the Rev. Richard Atthill made his appearance amongst us. He has been appointed to the living of Newmarket for six months, after which he will probably go home before entering on another cure. He brings word that the Dunsfords are in Peterboro; he had seen them there, but we did not get any very distinct account from him what our new neighbours are like; perhaps he would not prejudice us for or against. They are to occupy Mr. Atthill's house this winter.

1839

Extract from a letter from ANNE LANGTON, *dated 1 January, 1839.*

John and Mr. Wallis returned in due time from Toronto, having the promise that the business they went upon should be attended to by Government. John seemed very glad to be at home again after his several rambles, and we were not less so to see him again. We had never been so long left to ourselves before. He reported Toronto to be as quiet as if there were no war in the country—no bustle and excitement, as there was at this time last year. How one becomes habituated to everything, even to war and tumult. The number of military, however, had exhausted the city; nothing was to be had. There were no candles in the capital of the province. John, however, produced some window-latches, so that string and nails are dismissed from some of our windows. Our drawing-room was just completed before Christmas Day, and I assure you no little admiration has been bestowed upon it. I do not mean by guests, though no doubt they did admire; but it was from our self-satisfied selves that the exclamation "what a pretty room!" has burst forth, and a pretty room it most certainly is. The carpet looks uncommonly well, and it happens that the new hearth-rug we brought out suits it as if it had been made to correspond. We have had book-shelves put up on each side of the window, which come down to the ground, and without taking much from the size of the room they give us a very snug appearance. John's books as well as our own now adorn the room. The other bookcases we had a little lowered to admit of the busts being placed upon them. The *tout ensemble* gives great satisfaction. The Christmas party was not very numerous. Mr. Fraser had just got his "company," and Mr. Need, his lieutenant, was also detained by his military duties. The latter was here one day in the preceding week, not a little repenting his forwardness to volunteer his services. However, he is an idle man at present, and it is only proper that he should go and represent the Lakes among the defenders of the country. Half a dozen gentlemen only were added to our own party on Christmas Day, and the usual round and repetition of dinners during the week did not take place, though the friends concluded the last year yesterday with Mr. Dennistoun, and commence the one to-day with Mr. Wallis. Before this time next year one of the bachelor friends will have become a Benedict. Mr. Dennistoun's engagement to Miss Hamilton is declared to his friends. Miss Hamilton is at present at Peterboro. We asked Mrs. Hamilton to join the meeting on Christmas Day, but she declined, and indeed summer is, I think, a better time for ladies to visit each other in the country. I am, however, contemplating a drive down to the Dunsfords to pay my respects to the new-comers, and looking forward to the excursion with much pleasure. . . .

I intend now giving you a winter month, as I did an autumn one, and hope in the spring and summer to do the same. The two last months, November and December, were somewhat monotonous on the whole, affording no variety excepting in the domestic department, where variety is least of all agreeable. Our housemaid's place, vacated early in November, was, after a time, filled up by a little girl of fourteen, strong and stout, and very capable of being made a good servant, but she and our two older people did not draw well together. Of course both parties were in fault, and we were the sufferers from the inharmonious kitchen. The crisis, however, came, and the old people left us. I was sorry in some respects, for though not altogether suiting us, we might have gone on quietly during the winter months. However, the old woman was evidently tired of service, and, I daresay, now is rejoicing in the tranquility of her own shanty, and perhaps also in the absence of her husband, who has enlisted, and was certainly something of a tyrant. Since then our little maiden has had the assistance of one of Jordan's daughters for two or three weeks, but we are contriving now to do without any. Our former servant, William, resumed his duties for a time and his elder brother George is performing them now. Firing is a most troublesome part of housekeeping in this country, the drawing-in and cutting up of wood is endless. It is astonishing to see the piles that disappear in a day, but it must be so in such a climate as ours. Of course, this being our second winter, we are not expected to bear the cold quite as well as newcomers, but there are several reasons for our thinking more about it than last year. In the first place, the weather has been more severe, high winds have more generally prevailed with our sharpest frosts, and some of our rooms, too, owing to the shrinking and warping of wood, admit much more of the external air. My mother's room we had not the least difficulty in keeping perfectly warm last winter. The water very seldom froze in it, and never in the recess beside the fire. Now, within two or three inches of the chimney, which feels quite warm to the touch, our water becomes ice, and notwithstanding an excellent fire night and day the thermometer will remain sometimes ten, twelve or fifteen degrees below the freezing point. But this is on our colder days, and even then we have rarely been otherwise than warm in bed, though in covering we have never exceeded two blankets and the down quilt. I often admire the providential arrangement by which our blood continues to circulate when everything freezes about us.

From the journal of ANNE LANGTON *for January, 1839.*

Tuesday, January 1. I am presuming that my October journal was interesting to you before I receive any assurance to that effect, and purpose giving you a January one. . . . The first thing I saw on coming downstairs this morning was Sally Jordan milking the cows—where do you think? Exactly at the step of the front door; this is to enlighten you as to Canadian ideas of tidiness. I have seen all the sweepings from the up-stairs' rooms ornamenting the snow before the front door. This was what I saw; my first occupation in the new year was assisting in getting three plum-puddings into the pot, for we entertain company in the kitchen on New Year's Day.

Wednesday, January 2. The day has been so mild that I am in terrible apprehension of the January thaw commencing and interfering with our drive down to the Dunsfords, and if it does not take place this week, it will certainly not take place this month, and perhaps not this winter, for the accomplishment of it requires a combination of propitious circumstances. It is entirely the drive and not the call that I anticipate with pleasure. John returned from the New Year's celebration this morning, brought no news and no letter from England. . . . There never was such a dull Christmas known in the country, for there is no whiskey either at tavern or store, and the people are all sober perforce! By the bye, they sell at the store about 4000 gallons of whiskey annually, besides which most of the gentlemen get up their own separately for the supply of themselves and work-people. I had Menzies' two little girls for a lesson to-day. I have lately begun to teach them a little. They come for about an hour three times a week; as yet we are not all perfect in our letters, and I sometimes feel that, unaccustomed as I am to teaching, I shall not accomplish much in my short schooling. But one good effect it appears to have, that they get a little more teaching at home. I hope this may continue, and then my own efforts will certainly not have been thrown away. My pupils are two very pretty little girls about five and seven, and sometimes recall to my mind the dear little girls at Seedley. My mother was ironing and I cooking a good part of the morning, and maybe such avocations will mingle a good deal with our employments at present, as our little servant Kitty is quite by herself. She makes great exertions, however, when everything depends upon her, especially if cheered by a little applause.

Thursday, January 3. We have accomplished our drive

down to the Dunsfords, and this is a weight off all our minds. It was on John's as a thing that had to be done amongst other claims on himself and horses; on mine, as a thing that I was much afraid might, after all, not be; on my mother's as what perhaps might not be done without damage to her precious daughter, in the way of cold-taking, or being shaken to pieces, and the relief to Aunt Alice was that we took back to his own house her old plague "Mowbray," who had been an unwelcome visitor here for some time, preferring her unwilling hospitality (she is the dog-feeder) to his usual fare with his present master. The thermometer was high, and the snow quite too soft for very good sleighing, but as it will very probably be worse, we thought it best to set out. I felt a little like a child with a treat in prospect, and thought it was well worth staying at home for a long time to have a feeling so juvenile. John had often wished to drive a stranger on that road; he said I was not quite "green" enough, for though the thing was new to me, I had too good a notion of the general rudeness of the country to be duly surprised. At any rate, I am now enlightened, for he gave me an abstract of a sleigh drive, including in our eighteen miles more adventures than he had ever had in one journey before. Iron and leather gave way many times in the jerks they got, but the sleigh-driver on a bush road is accustomed to patching and piecing his harness. I have heard that it is positive pleasure to be thrown into the deep snow, and John also gratified me with an upset. I must say that the fall was soft and easy, but I was so enveloped in my long fur cloak that I scarcely knew how to get up again. . . . Our expedition occupied at the most six hours, including all detentions, and we must have sat better than one at the Dunsfords—I am now going to prepare wicks for candle-making.

Friday, January 4. Busy in the morning. . . . I shall spare you the details. In the afternoon I made, with a very little assistance from George, seven and a half dozen of candles. We have latterly made dip candles in preference to moulds, it is much more agreeable to have one good making, and have done for a time, than be filling your moulds every day. A larger number of dips than I made to-day would have given very little more trouble, but my candle wicks did not hold out. I have got eleven candles to the pound, and I look with much complacency at my performance. I did not remark yesterday upon the necessity there is of keeping your eyes open on the Bush roads. Many are the boughs and branches that, displaced by the horses' heads, come bounding back with double violence upon the occupiers of the sleigh, and sometimes a tree across the road requires your stooping very considerably to pass safely under it. Without constant attention you might get severely hurt.

Sunday, January 6. . . . John is gone up to the Falls this afternoon to be ready for the town meeting tomorrow morning. He is quite in doubt what to do about his journey to Peterboro, which should take place now. . . . There is very bad sleighing on the lake; in consequence of a great deal of snow falling before the ice was very solid there is water between the ice and snow, so that a very little real thaw would see the latter dissolved, and a fresh surface would be formed. This is of some consequence to John, for he purchased the crops at "Seringapatam" from Mr. Hamilton, and has at present upwards of thirty sleigh-loads of hay on the other side of the lake. One of John's objects in going to Peterboro now is to lay in provisions for summer. To the list of those already in store which my mother gave you has been added two pigs and another quarter of beef, and I hope shortly another fat pig of our own will be made into pork or bacon.

Monday, January 7. I cannot say that the thaw brings present comfort; it was almost one person's work for half the day keeping the water mopped up in the kitchen, as the joining of that lower roof to the house is not perfect.

However, there is an end of everything, even of the snow upon a house-top. It would take a much longer spell of this weather to reduce very apparently the ground's covering, but the stumps have all lost the "iced plum-cake" that sur-mounted each.

Tuesday, January 8. Freezing again hard this morning, to John's great disappointment; another day's thaw would per-haps have dissolved the wet snow on the lake entirely, and then the real ice would have risen to the top. Now there will be double ice again, and unless there is a good spell of frost before more snow the lake will be worse than ever. John walked home from the Falls this morning. I took a walk as far as the Dukes' to enquire after the baby, who had been an invalid, and to carry a small donation of clothing. It had rather weighed on my mother's mind that she had so few op-portunities for the exercise of charity, and she was somewhat pleased, I think, to hear that this family was a little com-plaining at being poorly off in some respects; but she had not had full satisfaction in her bounty, finding that they keep a servant. That should be a good land in which there is "neither poverty nor riches." My conscience has also been ill at ease on the same ground as my mother's, and I thought of commissioning you to relieve it for me, and asking you (my sympathies are all with the shivering) to lay out a couple of pounds in red flannel petticoats. Aunt Alice has been very busy trying to dye a white one blue, but it is **a failure.**

Wednesday, January 9. . . . I have been dipping into Laing's *Norway,* a book John has been reading with great interest. He thinks if the Yankees take possession here we must go to Norway. It seems, indeed, to possess some won-derful advantages; that of being nearer home is not a little one. At that distance one might almost make an annual trip to see one's friends in England.

Friday, January 11. . . . The most comfortable thing to-day is that I have a very nice baking, and there is nothing that affects the spirits more than the well or ill rising of your bread. Our servant of last year, Mary, blessed with most admirable spirits, if her bread would not rise was the most melancholy creature imaginable. I quite understand it, now that the bread is my department. I rather like it, and think that if I lived next door to a baker, I would not buy my bread. Though I continue to patronise hop-rising, I bake a little with leaven also, for if it escapes all sourness it is decidedly the best bread. My mother and Aunt Alice were busy, amongst other things, packing up some bedding against John goes down to Peterboro. The last time he was there he and Mr. Wallis hired a house, and intend to have nothing more to do with the Hotel. As they expected, some others of the neighbourhood have wished to join in the expense and the advantages, so that it is to become a sort of backwoodsman's club-house. The rent is fifteen pounds, the first year's rent to be laid out on a stable. There are four rooms and a kitchen. John and Mr. Wallis, as originators of the plan, intend to keep one room for their own exclusive use. They think that a man and his wife, for house-room and the use of the garden, will perform the services they will require, and on the whole expect that their visits to Peterboro will be made at rather less expense, and certainly with much more comfort than hitherto.

Saturday, January 12. Well! I had rather be a baker than a butcher. To-day's occupations were very much in the line of the latter. In the first place, we had all our shambles meat to take down and examine. The damage was not very considerable, but the trouble was. However, the dogs are all rejoicing in a full meal, and will live well for a week to come —it is an ill wind that blows nobody good. We also cut up a quarter of beef. John was operator in chief, but the saw and cleaver were also wielded by female hands. The kitchen scene would have entertained some of our English friends, and possibly shocked others. . . .

I did not get a tumble when I made one experiment of walking on snow-shoes, though rather near it two or three times. I once thought of having a pair, but I think the chances of my requiring them are very small. I have little to take me out at all, and still less off the beaten track. The lake is in very nice order for walking, but the poor horses in their journeys for hay break through sadly. They were over both yesterday and to-day, and upset both times.

Monday, January 14. A lovely morning, a moderate frost, thermometer 18, with a bright sun. There had been a sprinkling of snow, just sufficient to take the slipperiness from the ice. It looked very inviting, and John offered to take a walk with me. So, soon after breakfast I equipped myself, and we set off at a brisk pace in the direction of Sturgeon Point. I told John he must never expect his wife to keep up with him as well as his sister. It was delightful walking on the lake, something like Southport sands in their best days. We followed the track of some wolves, which must have passed in front of the clearing this morning.

Tuesday, January 15. Another brilliant morning, but severe frost. John had one trip for hay before breakfast, and afterwards took another walk with me—not a very long one. We bent our steps in the contrary direction to yesterday. The wolves and foxes had been enjoying themselves as well as ever; I shall begin to be acquainted with the tracks of the beasts of the forest. I looked back at our own tracks, and wondered whether mine would be recognised as that of a woman, enveloped as are my feet in two pairs of stockings, a pair of socks, my house moccasins, and another pair over them. My head also has a better defence against cold than a bonnet. I manufactured for myself a fur cap which comes down over my forehead and ears; otherwise, except on occasion of a sleigh drive, I do not wrap up a bit more than at home. John is mending his moccasins to-night, and it strikes me that a few glovers' needles would be a useful article to send us. He has filed a carpet needle for the present occasion into the proper angular shape. We are running short of large needles too; a paper of short thick ones, calculated to take a very strong thread, would be convenient.

Wednesday, January 16. I had a new pupil to-day, a little girl of the Daniels about ten years old. I scarcely yet know what her attainments are, for she is dreadfully frightened, and though she appeared to know scarcely more than her letters at first, I shall not think it all my own doing if I find that she can read at the end of a fortnight. I hope she will get some good from me, however, for she has nearly two miles to come for her lesson.

Thursday, January 17. . . . I have no incident great or small wherewith to make to-day's journal interesting. I shall be reduced to telling you what we have had for dinner. Our larder now allows plenty of variety in that meal. It is provoking that we should just have our best cheer at the season when we have no one to partake of it, and in summer, when we saw more company, and wished for something more than boiled or fried pork, we had to run the changes upon roast chicken, boiled chicken, hashed chicken, chicken rice, and chicken pie. I should say we used to get an accidental dish of fish when the Indians had been about. At present we do not shine much in the pudding line for want of eggs; and though our bread is super-excellent, butter at this season cannot be boasted of. By the bye, the Dunsfords laid in three hundred weight of butter for their winter supply, and consumed fifty pounds in three weeks. You see we gossip of each other's affairs here as elsewhere.

Friday, January 18. . . . We were quite aware, had John gone to England, that some of his friends would have wondered, and perhaps censured; and it seems that his brother would have been one of them. It would, however, have been all our own doing, my mother being the inventor and chief promoter of this plan. I still think if we, being pretty well, and feeling ourselves quite at home, and competent to manage all ordinary matters for ourselves, with willing friends at hand to assist us in case of extraordinary ones, should urge John to pay you two or three months' visit as our proxy, he should not be blamed for acceding to it.

Tuesday, January 22. My journal paused a couple of days in consequence of our excessive gaiety. On Sunday we, who have not had a caller since September, had two parties—the three gentlemen from Cameron's Lake, and Mr. Boyd. The former we regaled with rolled pig's head, bread and butter, and bun loaf, and let them depart. The latter we prevailed upon to remain to dinner and to stay all night but it was with some difficulty. He is a most resolute home-stayer and a very industrious settler, and has chopped all his own land himself. . . . There is to be a ball at Peterboro this week, but none of our backwoodsmen intend to go. John will be on the spot, but he said he should not go. I think he may perhaps change his mind when the time comes. There seems to be more spirit among the ladies at present; two of the Miss Dunsfords are going down thirty miles to attend this ball. Mr. and Mrs. Dunsford have announced their intention of coming up here as soon as their horses are at liberty (now engaged in bringing up their possessions); meanwhile they appear rather impatient for a sleigh drive, as they were on the lake the other day, pushed by their men. The Dunsfords have Mr. Need's book, so we have a chance of getting it. I am rather anxious to see what "the elegant and refined mind of the author" has produced. These words have nearly become a nickname for Mr. Need, but its inconvenient length will, I think, prevent it from permanently superseding the old one. . . . John thinks this will be his last visit to Peterboro this winter. We never ask him how long he is likely to be absent; it is much better both for him and us.

Wednesday, January 23. This is the very coldest day we have had. Our thoughts turned immediately to our traveller, and we hoped he had not to drive into Peterboro this morning. The thermometer was twenty below zero, with a strong wind. It blew very hard during the night; the mercury stood only three degrees above zero in our room whilst we were dressing. At noon it rose to five, and once we contrived to raise it to eight, which is the utmost a good fire has been able to do for it. I wanted my mother to remain in bed till after breakfast, and likewise to come down and dress by the parlour fire, where it is much warmer; but she will not be petted. The temperature of Aunt Alice's room is something higher than ours, but the thermometer fell there also to near zero at one time. It is the gable ends that are so dreadfully cold, being only of boards let into another like flooring, instead of logs and plaster; these shrink, and the lining boards also. Much of to-day has been spent in keeping ourselves warm, by which I do not mean standing or sitting over the fires, but going about piling wood upon them, and also with paste and brown paper seeking to keep out the cold wind. If I say much more I shall frighten you on our account. I must tell you then that the drawing-room is as warmable as ever, and the chimney does not smoke as it did last winter. When Aunt Alice and I were pasting up the wind-holes, my mother reproved us, saying it was ridiculous for people to come to Canada and not be able to bear a breath of air. She is determined not to be soft. All things are by comparison; after these frosts, when it is milder and I report the thermometer at nine or ten, my mother says, "Oh, dear! I am afraid it is going to thaw." You will perceive that all my thoughts run upon heat and cold to-day.

Thursday, January 24. The event contradicted my assertion respecting the thermometer in our room, for in the evening it rose actually to twenty, in consequence partly, no doubt, of the wind having fallen, and partly owing to our having lighted the stove in my little room, which has not been done before, and part of the partition being only boards, a good deal of warmth would come through. These stoves are invaluable in a cold climate; I do not know what we should do without that in the hall. This morning the thermometer stood out of doors at what it was yesterday in our room, in which it had now risen as high as eighteen, and the weather continues to become milder and we to think and talk less about it. We have had a little pig killed to-day, and are only waiting for a barrel of salt to kill a great one. This was school day; my new pupil is far in advance of the other children. My most distant scholars come twice a week, Mondays and Thursdays; the little ones likewise on a Wednesday, as they are close at hand, and it is worth while coming up for an hour. My mother's head is very rheumatic to-day: she keeps it well tied up.

Friday, January 25. I have spent almost all the day at John's, the latter part of it attended by Kitty, giving his house a good scrubbing, where I had been sweeping and tidying it beforehand. I came back with a strengthened conviction of the importance of woman, and congratulating myself, that though I might be an old maid I never could be an old bachelor. In summer we were able to send down every morning, that he might have his bed made, and things made a little comfortable for him. Now he depends upon the occasional visits of the ladies, and these are less frequent than in the milder season.

Monday, January 28. Another pause of two days, to be accounted for by the following details of them:—Saturday was one of the busiest of busy days. In the first place, we were both bakers and butchers, and the exercise of two such important callings filled up our morning. Soon after we had taken an early dinner arrived John from Peterboro, announcing two other gentlemen as on their way, intending to reach us to dinner. So forthwith another meal was prepared, to which, after waiting for our guests until near seven o'clock, we sat down alone. An hour or two afterwards the travellers arrived, hungry of course, so the board was again spread with a substantial tea, accompanied by pork steaks.

It blew fiercely all night and all the next day. After prayers on Sunday morning Mr. Fortye[1] and Mr. Ferguson resolved to pursue their journey to the Falls, but the road was reported impassable, so they remained quietly at John's cottage until we summoned them to dinner. Some hours were again spent in clearing away snow, and endeavouring to make the house comfortable.

My mother has just closed Mr. Need's book. It is a slight affair to have attracted so much notice, as from its mention

[1] Major Hamilton's son-in-law.

in the periodicals it appears to have done, and I think he has been well paid for the trouble of putting it together—it is something of a puff. John says he should like to get the book that he might send it to you with annotations. Our friend does not seem likely to redeem the character of travellers in general. His deviations from the undeniable, however, are chiefly in the spirit of book-making. Many little incidents, which serve to render the work amusing, could scarcely be produced at all except as extracts from a diary, where it is manifestly necessary that the first person must be used, and not the third.

Wednesday, January 30. We have just been inspecting number nine. Number ten, it appears, is still at Whitby, and we are informed that the bundle of down is lost. It reached Kingston, but has not since been heard of. Much as it is to be regretted, if we were to lose a package, there was scarcely one that could have been more easily dispensed with. At least it is but one thing, whereas if all the sundries that have been spread before us to-day had disappeared, we should have had a very extensive loss. However, we need not quite despair of it. One small parcel we had sent out to John was a year and half lost, yet appeared at last. . . . One thing the house most certainly is supplied with during our occupation of it, and that is pie dishes. They are just what we wanted; the tin plates, too, are very nice, and also the little tea-boiler, from the expedition with which warmth will be obtained.

Friday, February 1. I now close my journal until the 1st of April, when I intend to give you another peep at us. This month is ushered in busily. A pig was slaughtered to-day and my mother and I discovered that we are not quite perfect in our business yet, for the black puddings, which have rested with us for the first time, gave evidence of our inexperience. I am going to exercise my skill in shaping ham to-night. That I consider my special province. My mother shines in rolled pig's head, and Aunt Alice in pork pies.

From the journal of ANNE LANGTON *for April, 1839.*

Monday, April 1. I do not think this month, April, a very favourable one for the interest of the present sheet. John says it is the most disagreeable one of the whole year, because nothing can be done. But it is well you should see us in all our varieties. I will not be deterred from giving you my quarterly communication.

The roads are terrible at this season, the better parts of them somewhat reminding one of the dirty lanes near Blythe in the old world, whilst at other times one is indebted to some of the prostrate trees about for keeping one out of the deeper mire.

The Jordan family are busy in the sugar-bush, where Major Hamilton (who is still our guest) and I visited them and their boiling kettles. The sap runs beautifully on such a day as this. I counted the drops in a minute at two or three trees, and found them vary a good deal; the greatest number was 82. I drank a little of the sap in the most primitive of cups, the palm of my hand, and found it very cool and refreshing after a hot walk, though I thought it anything but pleasant when tasted under other circumstances. You who are an admirer of *eau sucrée* would, I daresay, approve. On our way we visited a family of newcomers, at present inhabiting Jordan's old shanty, though preparing one on their own land about a mile distant. Their name is Ingram, and they come from Ireland. I like to make you acquainted with all the *dramatis personae* of the place, and two of the junior members visit me three times a week— a nice smiling girl about eight years old, and a boy somewhat younger, with whom I am going over all the "a-b's and b-c's" that the others have done with. My other beginners are coming on very nicely.

Tuesday, April 2. We ladies have been exceedingly busy getting up our muslins, a very difficult operation with arrowroot as a substitute for starch. Do not imagine that the latter article it not attainable here, but we do not approve of its blackish-blue colour, and shall be glad to receive our supply from England.

Wednesday, April 3. Of a sleigh journey in the present state of the roads you cannot form any conception. It is marvellous how wood and iron hold together, to say nothing of bones, as you are tossed up and down, driving right over everything that lies in your way, even to the stems of prostrate trees occasionally. The snow makes all comparatively smooth, but there is very little left of it now.

Thursday, April 4. I purposed taking advantage of this holiday week to get well forward with work, but I have not done much. I made an attack upon my corsets to-day, however, and feel a little appalled at the difficulties before me. My mother and aunt have also been very busy preparing work in the upholstering line—sofa and chair-covers.

It is well for us to get forward with necessary work, for Mr. Wallis threatens to find us some occupation this summer in preparing for a bazaar—not to be held in this country, you may suppose. He talks of going home next winter, and in that case would get up a bazaar at Glasgow for the benefit of church and school here. I daresay such a thing would answer very well, and a few hundred pounds would do a great deal of good here. Population is increasing fast, and there must be some means provided for the education of the rising generation, or we may fall back behind the Indians. I am to send sketches of log-houses and shanties, etc. I wish our scenes were more beautiful. . . . We altered our breakfast hour for the summer this morning; now we assemble at half-past seven, and next week we begin dining in the middle of the day.

Sunday, April 7. The lake has risen very much, and now comes an anxious time for the pier. This is the third John has attempted, and if it does not stand, I think a fourth will not be tried, for everything has been done that can be done to make it secure. It will be a very great advantage to the landing, which is not a good one. There are no good ones on the lake. If it does stand, there is to be a boat-house in addition, which will also be a convenience, and, moreover, a great improvement to one of my contemplated sketches.

This winter chopping has made considerable alterations amongst the clearings to the back of us, but our panorama is very little changed. The butternut meadow to the right of our lake view is laid a little more open, and a few trees have been cut down on Dr. Diehl's land,[1] giving us a peep at the lake a little beyond the three tall pines. A much greater change, I hope, will be affected by the logging than by the chopping. John was just now wishing for fifty men and five yoke of oxen, but as he cannot have his wish, the wilderness of charred wood before us must disappear by degrees.

Tuesday, April 9. I am grieved to say the piers have given way to-day; there will be no boathouse this year, if ever, and the beautiful *Alice* must be exposed to the rays of a scorching sun. I suppose nothing will stand the force of the ice when it begins to move. I walked down to the lake to look at the damage. Within doors the day's proceedings have been highly uninteresting. I have been cutting open a pair of my new shoes, lacing them up, and concealing the lacing with a row of little bows down the front. If the novel appearance attracts attention, and I am asked if such is the fashion, I shall say I have just got them from England.

Wednesday, April 10. It has been raining heavily the greatest part of to-day, which will help the opening of the lakes. This event takes place rather early this year. The 12th of April is the soonest John has known it, the 7th of May the latest.

[1] Dr. Diehl's land, occasionally alluded to was Lot 15 in the Tenth Concession of the Township of Verulam. It was on the water front immediately south of the Langton water front and lay due west of the southern half of John Langton's property, between the high ground on which Blythe was built and the lakeshore to the west. The owner never appeared and his land was eventually sold to John Langton but it apparently continued to be spoken of as the Diehl Lot.

Thursday, April 11. What have I to record of this day? The bannisters have been put up, and we have been so long unaccustomed to anything of the sort, that when on the stairs we feel as if we were in a bird-cage. Rain came on again and put a stop to the logging, so the men came up to clean out our well, which makes a little confusion. In the kitchen it has been somewhat of a busy time this week. John's housekeeping does not commence until next month, so we have the men to feed, and only one domestic. That one, however, is Mary, a non-such in the way of getting through work—would she were everything else! Kitty, who will be back again in a few days, I fancy, is but a child, but I do not think many girls of fourteen would have done as well for us this winter as she has done. Not that her capabilities are anything very great except in the cleaning way, and she is a capital scrubber, and so stout and strong that one did not feel that a little hard-working occasionally would do her any harm, as one would have done with most girls. I much doubt her temper agreeing with any companion in the kitchen, and a second servant we are on the look out for. We are not equal to the same exertion in the heat of summer, besides which occasional bustles are more frequent.

Friday, April 12. This morning I thought there was as much ice on the lake as yesterday, but a breeze sprang up soon after breakfast and in a few minutes it had all floated down out of sight. There is not a vestige left, though I suppose lower down the lake will be still covered. John has been preparing his canoe for a paddle up to the Falls to-morrow. I hope he will bring down some letters. Aunt Alice is discussing her poultry yard whilst I write. It is her entire charge, and begins now to repay her care. She brought in eleven eggs this morning, but now is ambitious of having a dozen as the produce of a day. In winter we were two or three months without seeing one, but another winter the hens will be more comfortably lodged, and perhaps supply us better. The poultry here must suffer dreadfully from the cold. It is quite a common thing for them to lose their toes. One of ours lost an entire foot, though it contrived to walk about very well with the stump and the half foot that remained on the other leg. Some of the more weakly birds were frozen to death.

Saturday, April 13. This morning, in spite of a strong adverse wind, John set out in his canoe for the Falls. We watched him round the point, as we did many a time last year, and shall, I daresay, many a time this year. My mother felt a degree of anxiety on account of Cameron's Lake ice coming down the stream, so it was very satisfactory to see him land an hour earlier than we had expected his return. I have been engaged this afternoon making up my remaining store of tallow into four dozen portly-looking dips, eight to the pound. My last making was twelve dozen and I think the larger number is very much as quickly accomplished as the smaller one, for they gather more tallow when thoroughly cooled, so that with many I need not go through them so often as with few. Now that I know how to manage the matter I find it positively a cleanly operation. Mary looked horrified when I set up my apparatus in the kitchen, which had just received its Saturday polish, but I do not think she found it a bit worse when I had packed away my things again. The two elder ladies were still very busy upholstering. I do not think any ladies on the lake have better fitting garments than our two arm-chairs. As the fine season approaches we begin to think of the entertainments we must give to the newcomers. You would have been amused to hear John and me discussing the important subject this morning, asking each other with perfect solemnity, as if we had fifty to choose out of, whom shall we have to meet the Dunsfords? Answer—Mr. Wallis and Mr. Dennistoun. And whom shall we have to meet the Dobbs? Answer—Mr. Dennistoun and Mr. Wallis. We cannot have the ladies to meet each other owing to our limited accommodation.

Sunday, April 14. We have had changes in the household to-day. Mary has departed, and Kitty has returned to her place, bringing with her another girl, as she knew we wanted a servant. After some deliberation we engaged her for a month, though by no means promising to be all we wished in a servant. She is too young in the first place, only seventeen, whilst her companion is but fourteen or fifteen. But girls marry so early in this country, that a person of steady years is difficult to obtain, and one with any but the commonest sort of knowledge is quite out of the question. Perhaps this one may do as well as any other we should have got, though to you it must appear a curious way of engaging a domestic, simply on the recommendation of another. But here she was, some assistance we stood greatly in need of, with several work-people about, and some of John's valuable time will be saved by thus terminating the search.

Monday, April 15. John is off to Ops this morning, as also Mr. Wallis, both with their boats laden with sacks to bring corn out of Egypt. This day has been lovely. A coat of paint has been given to the exterior woodwork of the house, and the pump is put down in the kitchen, a perfect luxury after the slopping of buckets up and down a well. The first day of a new servant is always an uncommonly disagreeable day, and this has been by no means an exception, but I see no reason to think any worse of our speculation than I did yesterday. I have been just now engaged in killing mosquitoes on the windows. They come out early, which gives reason to hope that a sharp frost may make destruction amongst them. Last year at this time we had complete winter; now the cattle can pick up what almost keeps them. Good-night! We are just going to have some cake and wine in honour of your little two-year-old.

Tuesday, April 16. The important operation of laying out the grounds has commenced to-day. We have obtained a clever workman for about a week, but longer he is not to be had. Unfortunately workmen of any kind are hard to be met with at this busy season, or much might be accomplished in a short time under his direction. There will be some trifling alterations from the plan sent to you, of which you shall be duly informed. Spring-time makes busy work, notwithstanding the men and women about the house. John was to-day chopping firewood, I kneading bread, and the other ladies also busily occupied. This department of mine I intend now to resign, but to-day I had to pay the penalty of mismanaging matters so as to have to bake on a washing day. There is no unmixed good in this world. A wash-house, a boiler, and an oven are great comforts, but they consume an immensity of wood.

Thursday, April 18. Nothing at all narratable to-day but the progress of the mansion. We go up a step to the front door now, instead of treading as hitherto on a block of wood. The entrance looks quite handsome, but the rude substitute for the correct thing had ceased to look amiss in my eyes. To have a very graphic description of things in the backwoods it should be given by a new-comer, the inconsistencies and incompletenesses become too familiar to be observed. As an instance of the former, I will tell you that in Mrs. Dobbs' little drawing-room, which was very neatly set out with books, handsome work-boxes, and alabaster ornaments, there hung also a saddle.

Friday, April 19. We have seven men at work today; this looks like getting on. So many mouths make large bakings, and whilst superintending the operations at the oven to-day it occurred to me that a representation of it might add something to the interest of this stupid journal. Now I must go and see what the oven has been doing for me whilst I have been doing it so much honour. . . . It has returned the compliment very handsomely.

Sunday, April 21. We had a long talk about former days last night, sitting up to a very improper hour to do justice to the theme, and coming to the conclusion that not many families have had more variety in their life than ours. It is not a monotonous world, whatever other complaints we may have to make against it. We have another addition to our large family, for next week the kitchen party will be ten, so that our two girls, and the mistresses too, will be pretty busy. Our new damsel is by no means promising, and both have to be perpetually reminded. The more we do it, the more they depend on us, and the less again we trust to them, so that, like the vibrations of a pendulum, the thing is kept up *ad infinitum*. Such as ours, I suppose, is the ordinary sort of Canadian servant.

Tuesday, April 23. John set off to the Falls very early this morning, and returned towards evening with a scow load of trees. We shall begin to look quite umbrageous.

Wednesday, April 24. I have omitted to notice before the arrival of a blacksmith. We have had one occasionally at the Falls, but now he is permanently settled. As you have never sent a horse five-and-twenty miles to be shod, or waited three or four months for some trifling yet perhaps essential performance of the furnace, I cannot expect you to understand that an advancement in the settlement we consider the establishment of this worthy amongst us. There was a "Bee" to-day for making a road up to the church.

Friday, April 26. Last night I was so bent upon completing one half of my corsets, save the binding, that I did not take my pen in hand. You must think from my occasional mention of this piece of fancy-work that it is at least as tedious as a yard and a half square ottoman. But I have rarely taken my work out until after tea. Tea and candles generally come together, and then follows, or ought to follow, the journal, for if I put it off until later it often happens, as last night, then I get engrossed with my needle until the word is spoken, "We had better go to bed." At that time we move, but it by no means follows that it is to our beds, or even to our chambers. The change is frequently merely from a circle round the table to a semi-circle round the fire, and another half-hour or more passes before we really begin to go, after which an inspection of the larder always precedes the final departure. So you see we are very little changed. The scow-load of trees were planted yesterday, but make very little show. We mean to go on by degrees, planting a little every spring and autumn, and in time we shall have a very pretty place. To-day I was tempted by an abundance of eggs to do a little in the confectionery line, and have manufactured some biscuits in imitation of some square sweet ones that you may remember we used to patronise at Bootle. They say I have been tolerably successful.

Monday, April 29. I have omitted for two days to write my journal, not so much from the want of interest in the day's transactions as from the peculiar interest of the evenings which were taken up with the perusal of some of John's early letters from this country. I was amused with comparing the ideas they had led me to form with actual impressions. Although I was hopeful at that time, and John confessedly too sanguine in some of his views, yet could I have had a vision of the appearance of things five years later how thankful I should have been, and if I should have been so then, I hope I am so now. Draining and fencing are the present things in process, the ornamental pausing for a time. John has been constructing a novel form of fence to-day, rather more substantial than the ordinary ones in the hopes of preventing the intrusion of Aunt Alice's feathered friends. I am afraid her poultry yard and my mother's garden will not be on the most amiable terms. There was great alarm about the cattle last night— they had strayed into the woods. However, they had the bell with them, and were found this morning, but their milk will not be usable for a day or two.

Tuesday, April 30. I have contrived very well to make my thirty days occupy about the right quantity of paper, and I have just left what may serve to reply to the letter which we surely must have by to-morrow's post. . . . I have said little of my mother's occupations lately, for they have been very uniform. She has been determined to do her work very fully and completely, and, with some assistance from Aunt Alice, has manufactured a complete set of chair covers, sofa-covers, etc., and a second cover for each of the great chairs, besides refreshing all that wanted refreshing. Meanwhile I have been housekeeper-in-chief. Afterwards mantua-making must have its turn. Then we shall change places, and I shall preside at the needle. I must now take my leave of you until July, when I intend you to see something of our summer life.

May 1. My journal missed the post owing to a storm we had on Sunday, a sort of miniature storm it would appear to you islanders. Nevertheless it unroofed our root-house, uprooted sundry trees, carried the cover of the hot-bed to a considerable distance, overthrew fences, and might have been the destruction of the *Alice*. She dragged her anchor, but happily fastened again when not more than her own length from the shore. We watched her anxiously for a couple of hours in this perilous situation, when the waves were much too high to allow of a canoe going out to her even at that short distance. At one time John was just going to take his canoe for the purpose, when the wind raised it up, turned it two or three times over, and deposited it amongst stumps and stones, so that it got sundry awful holes in its bottom. Meanwhile hands had been mustered to the number of four, and, taking advantage of a lull in the storm, the precious *Alice* was placed in safety on the sandy beach in the bay, at the cost of a mid-way wetting to all and a complete ducking to others.

From the journal of ANNE LANGTON, *1839.*

Monday, July 1. The season has only just commenced; a week ago we were still enjoying fires, and notwithstanding our early spring the country is in a very backward state, owing to the long continuance of high and cold winds.

I am rather in expectation of a stupid month, partly because the last was a stirring one. I do not mean that we have been stirring, for not one of us has once moved from the clearing, but our little world has been stirring around us. We had last week a large "Bee." At our little one last year to raise the root-house we had some ten or a dozen men, but this time there were near forty, and seven yoke of oxen. Six or seven acres were logged up during the day. We walked down to take a view of the black and busy scene. One ought to see at what cost of labour land is cleared to appreciate even our bustled prospect. . . . There are four fishing lights on the lake to-night, which look very pretty moving up and down, but this holds out no prospect of a dish of fish tomorrow. The Indians find it more convenient to take their produce at once to the Falls where they have a certain sale for it. We are pulling very wry faces to-night at the mosquitoes.

Tuesday, July 2. We have been getting all our mosquito blinds into order; they have not been required hitherto, as there has been so little to induce us to sit with open windows. . . . We have had a thunderstorm to-day. My mother amused herself during the storm with repeating poetry, a thing I have not done for a very long time. The old world is the world of romance and poetry. I daresay our lakes, waterfalls, rapids, canoes, forests, Indian encampments, sound very well to you dwellers in the suburbs of a manufacturing town; nevertheless I assure you there cannot well be a more unpoetical and anti-romantic existence than ours.

Thursday, July 4. We all joined in a little tirade against Canada this morning, my mother's ground of complaint being the slovenly nature of its inhabitants, instanced by the scattering of lime and water over her flower-beds. Poor country! It bears the blame of all the various sins of the motley herd that inhabit it, besides the sins inherent in itself that it has to answer for. I grumbled a little at the necessity of storing all your summer provisions in the winter, and at the annoyance of unpacking and repacking barrels of pork, boiling brine, etc., etc. Our caterer I find, instead of a box of candles, has brought us a cask of tallow, much to our disappointment, having already abundance of work on hand. I have sometimes thought, and I may as well say it, now that it is grumbling day—woman is a bit of a slave in this country.

Friday, July 5. My mother and aunt preserved a quart of strawberries, which we have gathered in John's garden, whilst my avocations elicited another mute invective against pork and pork-barrels, after which I set about reducing the cape and sleeves of a gown to modern dimensions. Perhaps you may think this an unnecessary labour in the backwoods of Canada!

Sunday, July 7. The mosquitoes are sailing about in all directions, and make a great commotion against us, producing some exclamations, jumps, clapping of hands, etc. It is no joke to anyone to be so worried, but to my mother it is a very serious annoyance. The bites inflame exceedingly with her, and sometimes even produce something in the nature of prickly heat, but this I think is due more to the black fly than the mosquito, and most happily that insect does not often come into the house, so that by keeping a close prisoner you can escape it. The mark, too, of the black fly is much more disfiguring, resembling much a little leech bite, the first prick being less painful. The blood is sometimes streaming from you in various directions before you are aware that you are much bitten. You would not readily imagine the amount of resolution it requires to sit still making a sketch when the flies are bad. The mosquitoes will bite through almost anything, and the black flies are most ingenious in finding their way through all defences, and once within the folds of a closely tied handkerchief they do more mischief than if you had left them free access. If John takes up my journal I expect he will quiz my long dissertation on flies. He is often inclined to laugh at us.

Tuesday, July 9. Yesterday we had a piping hot morning, which made the culinary operations of the day appear rather formidable. Fortunately a storm came on, or rather a succession of storms, which, as they did not deter the guests from coming, suited us very well. These were Mr. Wallis, Mr. Jameson, Mr. McLaren, Mr. McCall[1] and Mr. Tom Fortye. This last is a brother of the Mr. Fortye who married Miss Hamilton, since dead. . . . The dinner served up to these illustrious personages was soup at the top, removed by (I am told) a very bad curry of my manufacture, boiled pork at the bottom, fried pork and ham at the two sides. Second course, pudding and tart. My biscuits, I presume, which appeared at dessert, were better than my curry: at any rate such ample justice was done to them that I am encouraged to give you the receipt—4 oz. of white sugar with as much water as will dissolve it, 4 oz. of clarified butter. This mixture to be poured hot upon 4 eggs, beating it up until a little cool. Throw in a few carroway seeds, and stir in as much flour as will make it into a *stiff* paste. Roll it and fold it as often as your patience will allow you. Bake it in cakes about the thickness of two half-crowns, which must be pricked. In the evening we had a card table. Miss Currer, Mr. Jameson, Mr. McLaren, and John sat down to it. The two young men entertained each other on the sofa, whilst Mr. Wallis, my mother, and I discussed various important and unimportant matters. Amongst the former were the flies in all their varieties, their attacks upon the human species, effects of the same, etc., etc., etc., as unfailing a topic, and much more inexhaustible, as the weather at home. . . .

My school assembled in the afternoon, but we all felt the weather. I was sleepy, and the children were languid. I had a new scholar, a girl of ten or twelve years of age, not yet perfect in her letters. And now I think my number is up. When more come on I must turn some of the old ones off, unless I can introduce the mutual instruction system, or, as I cannot well extend my school hours, the

---

[1] McCall had been an original settler on the south side of Sturgeon Lake, alongside of McAndrew and Macredie, thus completing "the three Macs," but he had given up his land five years before this and gone to New York. He was now paying a holiday visit to his old friends in the neighbourhood.

benefit to each individual must be necessarily diminished by an increase of numbers. At present if the amount of good gained in a lesson is not very great, at any rate they are put into the way of learning, and rendered capable of improving themselves.

Wednesday, July 10. After the regular duties of the day were over, I set about the manufacture of a bonnet for my mother, almost my first attempt in this line, for I do not reckon anything of covering one. My only other was the one I made last year for myself of lining calico, the whole concern worth a shilling or eighteen-pence, but it looked so respectable that I wore little else the whole summer. In the evening I went down to see the launch of the *Ninniwish,* a skiff John has built for his own single use.

Thursday, July 11. Our breakfast table was graced this morning with eighteen newspapers, and, what was much better, with five English letters, yours of the 11th June amongst them. As that part of the day not occupied by the perusal of these interesting despatches was dull enough, I shall devote a page to comment and reply. In the first place, do not send me out any portable musical instrument. There has been time and money enough already spent on me. The day may come when the first of these at least may be of less consequence than at present, and then I can make the experiment of how much music there is left in my soul.

I am afraid I shall not be able to send an old shoe, I never have any. The article is in great request among the servants, and my remaining pair of well-fitting ones are too precious to part with. I am not, however, so badly off in that department as I feared. Some of the boots and shoes I thought unwearable when my foot had been expanding in moccasins I can wear now. They tire me in the long-run but do not hurt, so I can wear them very well occasionally. Some I have disposed of, others altered to fit, so that the actual loss is not very great, and in case of failure this time I will try a new store at Peterboro, where, I understand, they have nice shoes—rather dear, I daresay. We have just packed a basket of prog for the gentlemen to-morrow.

Saturday, July 13. I take credit to myself for getting through twelve days' journal without once writing the word regatta, a sound which must vibrate on the air of these lakes some hundred and fifty times a day. On Cameron's Lake it has been the topic for the last three months. We are only just getting drawn in. The Regatta, together with the steamboat at the Falls standing still, and the ship-carpenters being unemployed, has led to the building of several new boats, and very much increased our navy. The merits, expectations, and adventures of the *Calypso,* the *Waterwitch,* the *Wave,* the *Coquette,* etc., form interesting variations to the theme.

Sunday, July 14. We had an exceedingly small congregation to-day, and it assembled very late. There is a difficulty in getting any regularity to an hour where there are no watches, or village clocks, or church bells. This I feel exceedingly in my school, but I believe it is an irremediable inconvenience.

Monday, July 15. I scarcely know what to tell you of to-day, except the last transaction of the day which was very unusual, namely writing a note of invitation. We have at last asked the Dunsfords for Saturday, thinking it would be a convenience, at least to the elders of the family, to find themselves so much nearer church on Sunday morning. The gentleman who will do the duty is only a deacon, therefore Mr. Dunsford will be asked to assist in order that the Sacrament may be administered.

Tuesday, July 16. My chief occupation was rigging myself up a morning gown out of one of my mother's, and making a collar to it out of superfluous sleeves. My mother handled the hoe instead of the needle, and was engaged for some time in trimming up her front garden.

Wednesday, July 17. John returned this morning. He

found Mr. Dunsford was gone to Toronto, therefore had not delivered our note, but we still purpose offering accommodation to some of the ladies. My mother was in her element to-day, tidying away the rubbish of the joiner's shop, the accumulation of ages. Miss Currer stuffed a pillow with feathers off the farm. The geese, however, were given up this year, they were so perpetually getting into the garden. I brought my gown to a conclusion, but am not at all satisfied with the performance. If, however, I have not succeeded in fashionizing the sleeves very gracefully, I have at least attained the object of the alteration, and got a neat little cape out of them.

Thursday, July 18. This morning, after sundry deliberations concerning the wind, and whether the southerly direction was likely to bring rain soon or not, it was determined that John and I should set out to carry our invitation to the Dunsfords. Accordingly I embarked for the first time on board the *Ninniwish,* and a very nice little boat it is, but I rather prefer a canoe for an expedition of moderate length. I don't know how I should bear the kneeling position for three or four hours in a canoe. I can take a paddle, and at least flatter myself that I do some little good, which is more agreeable than sitting in state at one end of the boat, and having nothing to do but observe my companion's exertions. But my canoeing days are over. John does not like the responsibility of taking me out in one, and thinks it altogether an unfit conveyance for so helpless a being as woman. I, having a due value for my precious life, should be sorry to urge the risk of it, but I am rather glad the idea did not spring up earlier. After we turned Sturgeon Point the wind was favourable. We put up a small sail, and proceeded more swiftly and easily on our voyage. It was the first time that I had been lower down than the Point since we came up—now almost two years ago. I think the lower part of the lake, upon the whole, superior to our end in point of beauty. Both shores are pretty, and the islands make an agreeable variety. Though at our end our own side is inferior to no part of the lake, the opposite coast is very monotonus. Mr. Dunsford's new house is a conspicuous object all the way down, and, I daresay itself commands a fine view, but it will be two or three months more, I fancy, before they will be able to get into it. We found the ladies luxuriating in the absence of all domestics, a variety of not unfrequent enjoyment in the backwoods. Their servant had taken her departure early one morning before the family were up, and since that the young ladies were taking it in turn to bake bread, make puddings, etc., and perform all the labours of the household. We can speak for the skill they have acquired in the first-named operation, for nicer bread was never laid on Canadian table than they placed before us, not even my own! After we had done justice to it, Mrs. Dunsford provided a further entertainment of harp and piano to enliven us during a thunderstorm. Our invitation was not accepted, which on some accounts I did not regret. We afterwards crossed the lake to Mr. Fraser's. He was absent, but we found his nice little wife at home and gave them the invitation just declined by the Dunsfords, which was conditionally accepted. Here, I saw and smelled the first roses since I came to Canada. Their little cottage is very pretty, with the wild vine and roses round the pillars of the verandah, and something more like a garden in front of it than can be elsewhere seen in these parts. We spent an hour or two very pleasantly with Mrs. Fraser. She is a very pleasing, unaffected person, and when we departed I wished she was nearer to us. Four hours' pulling against adverse wind brought us to our own landing just about sunset, and all the familiar objects about my home seemed to greet me with the same sort of old acquaintanceship as formerly after a long journey and an absence of weeks.

Monday, July 22. On Saturday we looked anxiously at the signs of the weather for the following day, and a fine one happily dawned upon us. About ten on Sunday morning two boats-full put off from the landing, and wended their way up the river to Fenelon Falls, and as soon as there was an appearance of the congregation assembling, we walked slowly up the hill to our little church. After morning service, at which from about eighty to a hundred people might be present, nine children were brought to be baptized, one or two of them about six or seven years of age, and afterwards one grown woman, who had officiated as sponsor to one of the children, came forward herself to be baptized. Being quite unable to answer the questions the clergyman put to her, he declined admitting her into the church at the time! Does not this show how much we stand in need of a regular minister amongst us? When this ceremony was over the time before evening service was so short that some of us preferred remaining in church to encountering another walk, and the gentlemen were so good as to bring up some sandwiches and a pail of water, which, with a little wine, was, I assure you, extremely refreshing, for we have now hot summer weather. Mr. Street,[1] who was very quiet and unaffected both in and out of the pulpit, and, moreover, pronounced by some of us to be very like you, William, gave us an excellent short sermon in the afternoon, and about five we re-embarked on our homeward course. What an event in our lives! and once we went to church every Sunday.

Mrs. Hamilton is going down to Peterboro on Wednesday she says, to scold her daughter for going out to parties and coming home at one or two in the morning, when the doctor has ordered her never to be out after sunset. Aunt Alice, who has often talked of a journey to Peterboro, though it was not clear whether in joke or in earnest, at length seriously determined to accompany Mrs. Hamilton, whose stay will be only a few days. Maggie Hamilton meanwhile is to be left with us. This was all settled yesterday, and now we must try to make out a long list of commissions, for my aunt will be rather lost in the great town without plenty to do. I believe she goes with an idea that she shall

---

1 Reverend George Charles Street, from Ancaster, later Canon of the Cathedral at Chicago. He was visiting the neighbourhood.

be able to get whatever she wants, in which I suspect she will be greatly mistaken. For my part, now that we have such a capital shopper to employ, I can scarcely think of a thing I do want.

We must get you to send us the notes of some good simple old psalm tunes. There is a book of such amongst my old music. I believe I oftener think of my music books than of my piano. Some dim recollection of an old favourite passes through my mind's ear, and I fancy I should like to see the notes. The psalm tunes, I hope, will be wanted soon for the church. Yesterday our carpenter was the leader, and several voices were joined to his. These, I hope, will increase in number and in power as we get accustomed to hear ourselves.

The church looks uncommonly neat now that it is finished, and would easily hold double the number that were assembled in it.

Tuesday, July 23. Miss Currer's courage has been cooling gradually all day respecting this Peterboro journey, at which I am not surprised, for the weather has been growing hotter and hotter. In the afternoon I received the agreeable announcement that a young woman was come to take our place. She had brought her bundle as usual, ready to establish herself, without the smallest doubt of being engaged. I was going to put a few questions to her, but seeing her very much heated I said she had better get her tea before we talked to her. Going out a few minutes afterwards, I found her with her hands in the wash-tub hard at work already. This looks well, and put a stop to all enquiries concerning qualifications, leaving only the simple one about wages to be made. How differently our domestic arrangements are formed here and in England!

Sunday, July 28. I have written no journal these several days. The fact is I am out of love with it. Either the month or I have been immensely stupid, and I begin to think the plan of making the day's transactions the subject of the evening's writing not a good one. However, as I have proceeded thus far in it, I will complete the month, without altogether breaking the thread of my narrative.

We had a visit from Mr. and Mrs. Fraser on Friday. They arrived just in time to partake of our early dinner. Mrs. Fraser appeared very shy when they were with us for the Regatta last autumn, and no wonder, after a five years' seclusion. Her winter at Peterboro, and a further acquaintance here, have quite removed the shyness, or at least only left what with her foreign accent and nice appearance makes her a very interesting little person. We hope to see them again at the Regatta. Mr. Fraser is very gentlemanly, and after seeing nothing but young men for so long, it is quite a treat to converse with a middle-aged one. We want decidedly an admixture of ages, as well as of sexes, to render our society what it should be. The pursuits and occupations, too, of all its members are too similar to afford much variety in the general run of conversation, and this defect I expect to be on the increase, as the varieties of our several younger years belong more and more to a remote past.

I fancy after four days' trial I may be expected to mention my hopes and my fears respecting our new domestic. I am sorry to say the latter greatly predominate. The only source of the former is that she is young and willing, but the height of her ambition seems to extend to acting by dictation. I must keep out of the way entirely in order to put her upon thinking instead of asking, "Shall I set the potatoes on now?" "Do you think there is fire enough on the bake kettle?" So far she has been small relief, and I am somewhat downhearted on the subject. Possibly she may be less lost and bewildered in a little time. This is the peculiar and unavoidable trial of the backwoods, and it colours the stream and directs the current of all one's ideas, and makes us very dull and stupid journal writers.

Saturday, August 3. We are once more in the midst of dirt and confusion, and surrounded by work-people. Happily, however, they are outside the house this time. We came to the decision of plastering the whole house, on account of the absolute necessity of doing something of that kind to the gable-ends to keep the cold out. We shall be much the better for this operation when it is over, but meanwhile the state of affairs is not the most comfortable, and the disagreeables attending it are on the increase. John was obliged to go down to Peterboro to provide nails and some other things for our proceedings. He set out at three o'clock in the morning on Tuesday, and breakfasted at home on Friday morning.

Mrs. Hamilton has had bad weather both going and coming—wet going down, cold coming up—so it was very well Aunt Alice had not joined her party. Moreover, Peterboro cannot at present supply the article she chiefly wanted, viz., crockery. Things will break here as elsewhere, and we want replenishing sadly. You have no idea of the extra value which glass, china, etc., acquire by removal to the wilderness. As for our candle lamp, it has become a perfect treasure, and we have as much care over it as if it were Aladin's own.

As this is not a letter, but a journal, I must give you something of the doings of the week. In the early part of it we were preserving ourselves a good supply of raspberries. It is a fruit we have in plenty, and much cheaper than in England. Pickling has also been the order of the day. We consume more in the way of ketchups, sauces, curry-powder, etc., than we used to do at home, on account of the many months we are without fresh meat. The latter part of the week I was making the discovery that I am no mantua-maker when out of the beaten track. I perplexed myself a little in the manufacturing of the black and white print you sent me out, but now when it is complete the performance is approved. It has, however, put it into my mind to ask you to send me occasionally, when there are changes, a bit of calico correctly shaped and properly plaited up into a sleeve. This is generally the most difficult and important part.

The new girl will not do. I never, I think, saw one so thoroughly useless. She is inconceivable and indescribable. We continue, however, to like her, and therefore must consider ourselves comparatively well off. Mrs. Hamilton cannot hear of a servant. She has only a temporary one, whose child she has also to accommodate. Mrs. Fortye was without one, the Dunsfords are without—all very encouraging! I hope we may succeed before the Regatta. I suppose Mary must again be our friend in need.

Mr. Boyd and Mr. Hamilton are dining here to-day with John as acting officers of the club, making preliminary arrangements for the great affair. Their deliberations appear to have provided me with a little more work, for the club is to give a flag for one of the prizes, which I am to design, if not in part execute.

Aunt Alice said in a very melancholy tone the other day, "I did think and say when we were coming to Canada, 'Well, there is one good thing in it, however, there will be no bazaars!'" Poor Miss Currer! She finds us much further advanced in folly than she expected. We have not only bazaars, but regattas! By the bye, there was a bazaar in Canada the other day, at Kingston, which produced the large sum of forty pounds.

Sunday, August 4. I will wish you, my dear Margaret, an ever joyful return of tomorrow. It will be your birthday and I welcome you to the top of the hill. John's toast to me on the 24th of June was, "an easy descent down the hill."[1]

Next to the biters our greatest insect pests are crickets. They are everywhere, and in such numbers that it is quite hopeless to attempt destroying them. Moreover they are very destructive. I find they have been feasting lately on my shoe leather. The noise of them at night is unceasing, but this we get accustomed to. There is a little beetle too, a great plague from its numbers, and a large kind of ant annoyed us a good deal last year in the sweetmeat cupboard. Beyond these we have nothing to complain of in the insect way. There are very few of the disgusting kinds which hot climates sometimes produce.

[1] Her 35th birthday. She died in 1893 at the age of 89.

From the journal of ANNE LANGTON *for December, 1839.*

Sunday, December 1. December finds us enjoying very lovely weather. It has been mild and sunny some days, but if tempted out by the external brightness, one finds one's expectations of a pleasant walk far from realized. This Fall has been very different from the last. We have had very few days of severe weather as yet. I know we mentioned the Indian summer in our last, but I am sure we did not half enough expatiate on the beauties of it. It prevailed during the greatest part of October, and very frequently until the last of the month we were entirely without fire, even at night. The lake has been frozen over about a week, at least our part of it. The ice came just one day too soon. We made an effort to get our packages out before the waters closed. John had two days journeying in miserable weather to make necessary arrangements. We had many changes of hopes and fears with the frosts and thaws during the period which must elapse before they would reach us. At length a beautiful thaw came, continuing a whole week, until the very day when we thought they might arrive. In fact they did come down the Scugog River, almost to the lake, when the ice became too strong, and they were taken back to Purdy's, there to lie a month or so until sleighing time.

Tuesday, December 3. I had my school today, but at present it consists only of my two oldest children. I do not regret it as these get a start from receiving more of my attention, whilst those I hope will not forget much who are at present kept away by bad roads and want of shoes. Schooling has been very light work for some time. First the harvest came, during which I had a very small attendance. Then the Regatta, which was a holiday. Afterwards potato-raising interfered a good deal, and now the roads.

I have been ironing a gown this morning, an accomplishment I have not yet perfectly attained, owing to the colour of our attire since we came; but though not yet quite at home in the operation, the result is very superior to what issues from the hands of our washerwoman. Our neighbours the Dunsfords have been living without a servant most of the summer, and the ladies have done all their own washing. They gain great credit for their exertions, and are themselves not a little pleased with them. I take it that an English lady transported here is ordinarily a more useful character than a Canadian-bred one. This I gather from what I hear, for of course I know nothing of it myself. Our clergyman's wife is a Canadian however, so I shall at least know one specimen. Mr. Fidler,[1] our pastor, I have just seen once. He is tall, middle-aged and gentlemanly. At present he has gone down to bring up his family. They have part of the tavern given up to them until a house is built. At all these arrivals of ladies I do not think I rejoice, as it would seem natural to do. I shall have to pay morning visits, etc., and I suppose I am growing savage, *alias* selfish, and unaccustomed to make sacrifice to society. What changes! Until the autumn of our arrival Mrs. Fraser had been the only lady in the settlement. Now there will be Mrs. Dennistoun, Mrs. Hamilton, Mrs. Fidler, Mrs. Hoare, ourselves, and all the Dunsfords in addition. There is another great alteration too. At one time Mr. Need and John were the only Englishmen among a considerable majority of Scotch and Irish. Now the Englishmen on the two lakes are eleven in number to five Scotchmen and four Irishmen.

Wednesday, December 4. What do you think I have been doing this evening? Taking a hand in a "rubber." I did so, I believe, that it might be apparent that my ignorance is real, and not feigned for the purpose of excusing me from making myself useful on other occasions. The Major[2] is fond of a "rubber," but among us of the upper end he is not often indulged, Aunt Alice and John being, I think, the only other whist-players—the lower-endians are rather more in that line. The weather is still magnificent. You have nothing like it in England.

Sunday, December 8. Notwithstanding the state of the

---

[1] This was the first incumbent of the Fenelon Falls church, which had been built three years previously. Up to this time services were held at rare intervals and by passing or visiting clergy.

[2] Mr. McLaren from Fenelon Falls, commonly called the Major.

roads, our congregation, which again assembles during Mr. Fidler's absence, was an excellent one. We numbered twenty-one. John being away, I was parson, and took my text from Romans ch. xiv. v. 16. Whilst rejoicing in the advantages of a regular clergyman and place of public worship, I feel some regret that this little assembly of neighbours must cease. Some of our party will certainly not be able to get to church during the winter months, and even I, who have been somewhat too tenderly bred for a backwoodswoman shall be a little dependent on weather. When once sleighing begins there is less to interfere with moving to and fro than in the summer season, when wind and water are the creatures we have to deal with.

Tuesday, December 10. John came home yesterday reporting that the house for our clergyman is begun. It is to look on to Cameron's Lake, will be close to Mr. Wallis's, very near to the village, but almost half a mile from the church. We are all mustering our forces to provide a comfortable dwelling for our pastor. The labouring classes give work, and the moneyed settlers cash.

I look upon the transactions of the neighbourhood which concern me not still with something more of interest than I felt in the ordinary ones of any other neighbourhood I ever lived in. I never felt before that I was in the least likely to be permanently settled. Now, though I cannot estimate the probabilities of the case, I think it is very possible I may live and die where I am, and the thought sometimes crosses my mind in looking round on the younger part of the population, will there be anybody to care for the old woman at Blythe?

John is gone to-day to blaze[1] a road through the forest to Mr. Boyd's. It shortens the distance there by half, and brings all that part of the lake above five miles nearer to us. My mother is very busy at present preparing some red cloaks wherewith she intends to make all my school girls happy this

[1] Mark trees to be felled.

Christmas. They will look most snug and comfortable. Good warm clothing is very dear in this country, and not easily attainable by the poor settlers. Yet notwithstanding this, I believe there is much more suffering from cold in England than here. The forest is always at hand, and those who have only one room can have little difficulty in keeping warm, though where they are multiplied by the necessities of civilisation, it is not only extremely expensive, but a great inconvenience to have to perpetually consider your stock of firewood, and almost impossible, as other things have to be attended to, ever to get sufficiently beforehand to feel at rest on the subject for any length of time. And so we have, as is quite right, to pay the price of our comforts and refinements.

Friday, December 13. Nothing remarkable to-day excepting that we hung our first bacon, six hams now in pickle will soon decorate our kitchen. It is John's ambition to see it adorned by twenty flitches and twenty hams, but the pig department is not very flourishing at present, as we are killing off an indifferent breed.

Saturday, December 14. We have a great addition to the premises lately in the shape of a wood-shed. The cattle have also had a new building bestowed upon them this fall, which, until you get a new sketch of the farm, you must remember is situated half-way between the stable and barn.

Wednesday, December 18. Yesterday brought us a little more variety, first in the shape of a note from Mr. Dennistoun, requesting John's attendance on the 24th,[1] so the important subject of the wardrobe had to be discussed, and the ways and means of travelling, etc. As regards the first of these subjects of consideration, a certain brown coat which appeared at Margaret Earle's wedding, and at your own, is to come forth once more on the present occasion, and the other points of equipment were satisfactorily arranged. But travelling, unless the roads greatly improve in the next week, will present many difficulties and inconveniences. There is

[1] The day fixed for his marriage to Miss Maxwell Hamilton.

but little snow, and no ice that can be trusted. In all probability the bride and bridegroom, who intend going to Toronto before they return, will have to perform part of their expedition in a waggon. A romantic excursion truly! and one would think very little fit for a delicate person to undertake. John is very sorry that his presence was asked for, and everybody thinks a most inconvenient season has been fixed upon.

In the evening Mr. Hamilton and Mr. Alexander Dennistoun arrived before tea, and spent the evening with us. The envious young bachelors, who had no wedding prospects, were very much inclined to laugh at the happy man who has. They quizzed his great and active preparations for the event! It appears that he has as yet got scarcely anything into the house, and with these roads Mrs. Hamilton must be quite cut off from rendering assistance in making things a little ready. The bride will find plenty of occupation and amusement when she comes herself in making all comfortable. Another subject of mirth was that there has been no wedding ring provided. Peterboro cannot furnish one, and they think one will have to be borrowed.

I find your opinion respecting our regatta coincides with some of the wiser heads here. The number of wise ones, too, seems very much increasing, so I expect you will hear of no more regattas. I believe the backwoodsmen were very glad of an occasion to ask their friends up here, and make some return for the civilities they receive at Peterboro, and for once or twice I have no doubt pleasure was afforded, but it would be too much to expect them to visit the back lakes again and again.

Thursday, December 19. This having been school day I will make it the occasion of thanking you for the little book you have for me. I have no doubt that were you, or your friend Dr. Kay, to visit my school you would find great occasion to reform it. I go on in a hum-drum old-fashioned way, teaching just reading and writing, and very little else. . . . I am quite sensible that the instruction I give goes a very small way indeed towards complete education, and I have felt a misgiving lest, in some cases, the fact of a child being sent to me for two or three hours twice a week affords an excuse for neglecting it at home. I endeavour to impress it upon their friends that I by no means charge myself with the whole education, but am willing to give a little assistance such as may be in my power. In one case, where they are very competent to teach at home, I very much question whether my assistance has not been worse than useless on this account. One individual has actually made it an excuse for not doing anything towards a schoolhouse that he could send his child to me. In other cases, however, I must do some good, though the amount of it may be small. In one neither the father nor mother can either read or write, though evidently in many respects quite better sort of people, and their children show more complete cleanliness and propriety than any others. In another case they are a very large and busy family, and have made some small effort towards instruction themselves, though they complain that the children lose in the summer what they can teach them during the winter months. They evidently value instruction, and rarely have kept their daughter at home, though she is at a very useful age. I have only to complain in one instance that the benefit afforded is not appreciated, at least that a very irregular attendance is obtained. But I should not talk of appreciating the benefit when I was just going to tell you how small it was after all. Most of my scholars have to begin from the a-b-c, and until a little reading is accomplished I scarcely think, with my limited days and hours, I can attempt anything beyond it. Writing I began with the elder ones, merely by way of occupying profitably the time in which the others were saying their lessons, but to very little profit did they use the pen until latterly, when from a smaller number I have been able to give more direct attention to it, and decided improvement begins to appear. With my readers I am at present pleased enough if they appear to take in the direct meaning of the words as they read them, without entering into any explanations or questionings that may help to open their understandings. I do not know what progress can be expected from children who say a lesson twice a week, and perhaps never look at a book at any other time.

Sunday, December 22. Friday and Saturday were rather busy days, the extra work that made them so was fitting John out for his expedition, not exactly for the wedding, though my mother ironed his shirt for the morning, and wished she were beautifying him for his own wedding. We were also providing for his comfort during the journey, knitting gaiters to keep the snow out of his moccasins. With these roads he may expect to have to jump out of the sleigh some twenty times, and I hope our performance will prove useful.

All sorts of defences against the weather are of great importance here. My mother accuses me of not wrapping up. What do *you* think? At the present moment I am wearing two pairs of stockings, a pair of socks, a pair of shoes, and a pair of moccasins. . . .

We are going to lose one of our neighbours in consequence of his wife not being satisfied with solitude. John's comment on the matter is that a man runs a great risk when he marries in this country. I think it is one thing that keeps our backwoodsmen so long unmarried. The risk is by no means obviated by taking a wife of the daughters of the land. Indeed, those who have been accustomed to the semi-civilisation of the more settled districts have a much greater horror of forest seclusion than such as have really lived in the world. I think the nuptials at present proceeding have brought the old topic more into my mind. I believe John begins to give himself up, so we may jog down the hill together, sympathizing with each other in our forlorn condition.

One circumstance has occurred to-day which I have no pleasure in recording. Our servant has given notice of her intention to return home. It is the same one whom we have had since May last. I had got accustomed to her, and liked her for many things, not for any astonishing capabilities as a servant. Our boy is clever, and at present his laziness does not interfere with our comfort, for if he does but keep the house supplied with wood, the pathways clear of snow, the poultry fed, and the plate and knives cleaned, we have nothing to complain of, though perhaps fuller occupation might be better for himself. It is on the strength of Margaret's invitation to enter into domestic details that I have said so much.

Candle-making, both moulds and dips, was the order of the day a little while ago. I wish I could have an hour's conversation with a tallow-chandler. Can you procure me some hints concerning the business, as to the temperature of the room, temperature of the tallow, etc.; what can prevent a dip from being thicker at the bottom than at the top? Also look at one properly made and tell me how near the wick reaches to the bottom of the candle.

Monday, December 23. Active preparations for Christmas commenced to-day—raisin-stoning, sugar-scraping, etc., had been accomplished before, but some of the good things were now put together, and we deal much more largely in them than we ever did before. Our carpenter arrived this evening and we held a consultation on the making up of my footstool. I hope he will make a good job of it. I was considerably perplexed in the manufacture of a cord for it. At last I accomplished a neat one, with appropriate coloured braids wound round a strong string.

Wednesday, December 25. Of course, without sleigh and sleigh-drivers we could not go to church, and the absence of the congregation which used to assemble here has made the day completely different from what it was before.

Sunday, December 29. John and the other wedding guests got back just in time to assemble round our table on Friday. All had gone off very well at Peterboro, though the ring was really a borrowed one! The ladies in attendance and their dresses have been all duly described to us, also that of the gentlemen, from which it appears that very few of the latter wore their own clothes. This may surprise you, but not those who know to what extent the system of borrowing and lending is carried here. Wardrobes are often scantily furnished, and, moreover, the young men move about unencumbered with carpet bags, and trust to each other for the necessary changes. It not unfrequently happens that three or four of them dine here, all more or less equipped in John's clothes. On one occasion Mrs. Hamilton, being in quest of some stray articles of her son's wardrobe, took the liberty of inspecting the linen of a young friend as it issued from the hands of his washerwoman, where she found every single piece was marked with another name than his own.

1840

From the journal of ANNE LANGTON, *for March, 1840.*

Sunday, March 1. I hesitated to-day whether I should not postpone my journal until a more promising month, but I have resolved to let you take your chance, though I very much fear two-thirds of it will be filled with comments on the weather, at least if they bear the same proportion to it that the subject does to all our thoughts and conversation. It is really one of supreme importance, and I reconcile myself to satiating you with it from the idea that it is characteristic of the country, where both in summer and winter we depend so entirely upon it for our roads, etc. I recollect saying in my last that the horses were to be busy all February drawing in firewood, so little did I know about the matter. We have had throughout it nothing but a succession of thaws, so that scarcely any snow now remains on the ground, and the whole month it has been scarcely possible to accomplish anything. John has employed his horses a little to bring up lumber from Bobcaygeon. We are going to try to accomplish our call upon Mrs. Dennistoun tomorrow. As she has been married upwards of two months this would seem rather extraordinary to those only accustomed to the facilities of the old country. I have only got three times to church as yet this year, which seemed unaccountable even to ourselves until we looked back, and observed how Sunday after Sunday some impediment arose.

Monday, March 2. We have had a brilliant day for our

expedition. When the snow first departs it reveals many blemishes that one had almost forgotten, and I thought the village at the Falls looked almost more wild than ever to-day. In the clearing sleighing is now very bad, but there is still some tolerable road in the bush. With all the shaking of bush travelling I think it exceedingly pleasant, and infinitely preferable to skimming along the surface of the lake, which in the long-run would become exceedingly monotonous. There is a great deal of variety in the details of forest scenery, and I think it would be long before the peculiar beauties would cease to excite pleasurable sensations in me. In returning we called on Mr. and Mrs Hoare. They are now in possession of Mr. Jameson's house and farm. I am glad to have a few more elderly people amongst us; we want variety.

Tuesday, March 3. John made an expedition to Bobcaygeon to-day for lumber. The ice was very good in the morning, but very soft at night. He invited some of the gentlemen from the lower end for Thursday, to help to eat up some of our provisions. We had very little fresh meat all winter until John's last visit to Peterboro, when for the first time he had the means of bringing up a load, and accordingly stocked our larder with a quarter of beef and half a sheep. From that time the thaw set in, and it has required great contrivance not to lose much of the enjoyment of these luxuries. We had a pedlar here to-day, the first incident of the kind since we came into the country. His goods were all in the tin line, and we resolved to make a purchase by way of encouragement. I think he received such very effectually, for the shining metal proved very attractive, not to ourselves alone, but, luckily for him, to a neighbour who happened to be there.

Wednesday, March 4. The chief incident of the day has been the departure of our servant Bridget. She had been with us between nine and ten months, something longer than any other we have had. Her deficiencies were many, but she had some good points for which I regret her. My mother thinks that I have led you to suppose that we have had a little more leisure this winter than the last. You must take a little to mean a *very* little, the whole amount at any time is but small. Our friend in need, Mary Scarry, is come to us to-day to see us over our party to-morrow, after which I suppose she will go back to the sugar-making, and we must get Sally Jordan as a help until we get a servant. I begin to think that those lead the easiest lives who keep no servant, and can simplify their housekeeping arrangements accordingly. Mrs. Fraser and Mrs. Fidler are the enviable ones at present. The Dunsfords have been multiplying their cares, for they are keeping three servants now, and I am afraid are raising wages. John made another trip to Bobcaygeon to-day, but I think it will be his last, for the ice is getting baddish. There are some amusing love affairs going forward at the lower end, which give great entertainment to the two old bachelors (Mr. Need and John have lately acquired that character).

Friday, March 6. The day went off very well. The cooks performed well, the waiter performed well, and the guests performed well, doing justice to the entertainment, and laughing and talking very merrily. They were Mr. Need, Mr. Dunsford junior, Mr. Jones, Mr. Edward Atthill, Mr. McLaren, and Mr. Unwin, a resident at present on Pigeon Lake, and a visitor here for the first time—a very grave, quiet personage. He rather contemplates settling on this lake, but I think not at our end. The large family of young people below, all full of gaiety and enjoyment, give a somewhat different character to the society there. We are much more sedate at this end, as may well be, for though pretty well evenly divided as to numbers, I daresay our united years are little short of double theirs. We are sometimes amused to see the youngest member of our family looked up to and made the confidante and adviser of so many juniors.

The whole party were with us again at breakfast, after which a sleigh load descended the lake. The ice is very doubtful. John broke through on his trip, and how his horses scrambled out he scarcely knows. Their hind legs were drawn in up to the rump, and he himself thrown upon their heels, but the sleigh never actually stopped. Its impetus, I suppose, materially assisted the horses in extricating themselves. The worst result was that John got very wet, and has a cold in consequence. I am glad to say he has nothing to take him on the ice again.

Sunday, March 8. The wind blew through John's house so much that he came to nurse his cold up here, and I am sorry to say it seems to require more of such treatment than his colds generally do. To-day, in consequence, we spent our Sunday at home. I have just finished a pair of screens as a wedding present to Mr. Wallis.[1] I think the performance very successful. They are on wood, in the old style, but a little more brilliant in colour than former ones. I have adopted turpentine and varnish instead of watercolour for my border, and the colouring-matter is no other poses.
than the powder blue you sent us out for less elegant pur-

Tuesday, March 10. I got my candle-making over to-day, and now I have only to fill the moulds a few times, and I shall have made up my half-cask of tallow. Ten dippings made very respectable candles to-day, whereas what I was obliged to make in summer after four-and-twenty were most miserable pig-tails.

Wednesday, March 11. The improved roads brought Mr. and Mrs. Dennistoun to return our call to-day. I rejoiced that they did not break in upon my candle-making yesterday. A small luncheon of cold ham, bread and butter, and a bun loaf was their entertainment. This party was scarcely gone when Mr. Wallis arrived to engage John to go down with him to Peterboro, and possibly to Kingston, but that will not be known until they reach the former

[1] He was married to Miss Janet Fisher at Kingston in the following May.

place. It appears that there has been a little playing at cross purposes. In this "affair" John has been the confidant and adviser.

Thursday, March 12. I presented my screens to Mr. Wallis, incomplete as yet for want of handles, which neither Toronto nor Kingston could furnish (what a country!), and the travellers were soon on their way. I have been again trying to drive a little intelligence into the untutored children of the forest. I have somewhat enlarged my system of tuition, and another branch of knowledge will be added to their extensive acquirements! I get assistance from my mother and Aunt Alice; the former has taken one little scribe entirely under her superintendence, and the latter often hears one or other of the reading lessons. Mr. Fidler has twenty-eight pupils, some much more advanced in years and accomplishments than mine.

Sunday, March 15. The bright sunshine took my mother down to John's house, which generally has a visit from us during his absence to receive a little extra dusting. Aunt Alice the most frequently walks down to it, being chief superintendent of his wardrobe. The roads are very indifferent at present. Mr. Wallis got an upset the other morning coming down, in going through a mudhole. We cannot afford to spend much labour upon road-making in this country. The trees cannot be cut down close to the ground. When there is plenty of snow the low stumps are covered, but as it disappears more and more skill is required in keeping clear of them and of other hindrances. John is a very clever driver. The Sunday evening amusement of reading old letters is not yet exhausted. We perused a year's correspondence to-day, dated Mount Pleasant, where such a tissue of domestic troubles was recorded as made one well satisfied to suffer here chiefly those arising from ignorance, and other deficiencies incident to a wild uncultured education. I say chiefly, for the human soil is full of all sorts of weeds here as elsewhere, but many are necessarily stunted in so rigid a clime which thrive most luxuriantly in the hot-bed of a large city. At home, there being a class regularly educated for service it gives good facilities on the one hand, but on the other that class forms a sort of party, constantly striving for its own interests in opposition to those of the party it serves. The very circumstance of difficulty in procuring servants, too, tends to make one more willing to endure trifling imperfections. You take them in a measure "for better for worse," and in some degree the happy results of an indissoluble connection may ensue. Our little damsel of last winter is now living with Mrs. Hamilton, and, I understand, in favour. She has no fellow-servant now, which will suit her peculiar disposition better, and powers she certainly possesses.

Monday, March 16. I was pleased to hear the following little circumstance from Mr. Fidler. Half a dozen of his elder scholars of their own accord brought their axes with them one day, and as soon as school was over betook themselves to the wood, borrowed a horse and sleigh, and before night brought in several loads of fire-wood, and piled them up at his door.

Tuesday, March 17. We had a misfortune this morning. A ham we had put to smoke down the chimney got somewhat over roasted, so that the meat slipped out of the skin and came tumbling down upon the fire, all broken to pieces, of course, but we got a little savoury picking out of it. We have been rather famous for our hams hitherto, but I am afraid we shall fail this year, both in quantity and quality. We got through our ironing to-day, and the starch performed very well except for chapping my hands a little. They have escaped altogether this winter, owing to my wearing mittens very constantly.

Thursday, March 19. We have been trying to concoct legs of pork from the pickle tub into hams. I manufactured a few sweet biscuits, and my mother rummaged over places that had got a little out of order. She is preparing for a grand scouring, of which you will probably hear to-morrow.

The roads must be terrible for a bridal party. I went down to John's, and almost stuck fast at each step in a glutinous mud.

Friday, March 20. The details of to-day were anything but pleasant; the result, however, is very satisfactory. We got Sally Jordan to come and give her assistance, and we ladies were as busy as the servants, rubbing furniture, etc. Not, however, busier than we have been on a like occasion at Bootle. Here, indeed, we may make a comparison in favour of this much-abused country. You lose no respect by such exertions. In Mount Pleasant, where our establishment was very small, we used occasionally at busy times to make our beds. On one occasion a house-maid, receiving her dismissal, was inclined to retaliate by a little insolence, and told us we certainly were no ladies, or we should not make beds. Here one of our domestics would be surprised, and perhaps think herself a little ill-used if, in any extra bustle, we should be sitting in our drawing-room. They are apt to think it quite right that we should be taking our due share, and are certainly our "helps," though we do not call them so, as in the States. I cannot perceive that anything like disrespect is engendered by this relative position of mistress and maid.

Sunday, March 22. I was prevented taking out my journal last night by the arrival of our two travellers John and Wallis. There will be no bride, it appears, for two or three weeks longer. The gentlemen were at Cobourg, undergoing together the agreeable operation of tooth-drawing. That there should have been an expedition at all in an uncertainty about the marriage must appear strange on your side of the water. But when you consider the state of the post in this country, where three weeks might easily elapse before an interchange of letters could take place, circumstances may be conceived to render it necessary. The Bishop's letter from Toronto about the grant to the church arrived ten days after date; had it required an answer six more days must necessarily pass before one could be despatched, which might be two more on the road. Intercourse is slow and uncertain to a degree quite unknown in a land of mail-coaches and macadamised roads. All the news the travellers brought home related to the present prevailing topic. If I were to give it to you I should get quite too gossiping. Even the public news is about marrying and giving in marriage, the Queen's wedding being the latest arrived.

Friday, March 27. Unpacking and repacking barrels of pork, and boiling pickle made this a busy day, and there is more of the same sort to do to-morrow. Not so, I am happy to say, with regard to what has been of late a daily occupation, for I have put the last tallow into the moulds. I begin to feel ashamed of recording these household occupations. You have had enough of them to form an idea of how we go on, so I think I shall drop these vulgar matters in future journals. We had a begging petition to-day, the second only since we came into this country. The former one was on the occasion of the death of a cow; this was on the levy of a fine with costs for selling whiskey without a license. Every one seemed disposed to open their purse-strings, for though the man, of course, was wrong, his case seemed hard, because the fining magistrate is a tavern-keeper. Law is rather curiously carried on in this irregular country. On one occasion damage had been awarded, and the jury gave in some curious sum, ending with odd shillings, pence, and halfpence. It was proved that they had not been able to come to an agreement what the sum should be, so struck an average of the different amounts advocated.

Sunday, March 29. I omitted to tell you that the Bishop promises to advocate Mr. Fidler's cause with the "Society for the Propagation of the Gospel," so I hope he may receive the full allowance of a hundred a year, which is their usual grant.

Monday, March 30. We have to-day most particular cause to be thankful; John's house has had a narrow escape of being burnt down. Yesterday afternoon John's man,

William Ellis, set out to walk with our carpenter to Jordan's, but after going part of the way changed his mind, and turned back, and also just stepped by chance into John's house. The floor had taken fire, and one of the beams was quite burnt through. The first was soon extinguished, but a very short time more might have made a very difficult case of it. When a log gets burnt through and breaks in the middle, the parts often fall asunder with some force, and scatter fragments far and wide. Such, most probably, had been the case now, and had not the man turned back John would, in all probability, have returned this morning to find his little home a heap of ashes, and all his clothes, papers, and valuables of all sorts consumed. It frightens one to think of it only. In what consternation we should have been. There is something awful in these wooden habitations, especially after one has seen one ablaze. There was a very considerable fire a short time ago at Peterboro. To be burnt out is a very common occurrence here.

From the journal of ANNE LANGTON *for June, 1840.*

Monday, June 1. A week ago we were so little satisfied about Aunt Alice that we despatched our youth down to Peterboro for the doctor. But regardless of the ten dollars that would have been his he has not attended to our call, and happily, it appears, we shall do without him. Early last week John went down to Peterboro to attend a meeting of magistrates but on Friday he returned, rowing up Mr. and Mrs. Wallis and accompanied by Mr. Atthill who has at length made his reappearance among us. We have just been despatching an invitation to the Dennistouns for Thursday—I hope they will come.

Tuesday, June 2. Our invitation was accepted, and just as we were pondering upon the best method of manufacturing a top, bottom, and four corners out of pork and poultry, arrived a present of veal from Mrs. Hoare. No hare or pheasant ever arrived more opportunely than did this rarity, unseen here for two years. It has set our minds at rest so completely that we have not again discussed the arrangement of our viands. I must try to brighten up for the occasion, but I feel myself fast approaching six-and-thirty, little less than double the age of Mrs. Dennistoun. I daresay the voices of the Miss Dunsfords are again enchanting them this evening, and that bad weather for once has been rather welcome than otherwise.

Thursday, June 4. A few preparations were made for the coming entertainment. The day was pretty fine, yet brought us no tidings of our gentlemen. My mother got a little fidgety towards night. However, they reached the landing, accompanied by Mr. Boyd, early in the morning. I perceived them as I stepped out of bed, and they arrived to breakfast. Having made our room ready for Mrs. Dennistoun, I slipped from under my mosquito curtains, and counted eleven bites upon my face only. I shall be a beauty to-night.

Friday, June 5. The dinner prepared was soup at the top, removed by a boiled fillet of veal, pork at bottom; corners, spring chickens, ham and veal steaks, and maccaroni. Second course, pudding, tart, trifle, and cheese cakes— a small party, and some of our luxuries were reserved for luncheon to-day, when we expect two boats-full of Dunsfords, coming up to pay their respect to the bride at the Falls.[1] When we, who had worked in sight of each other all day, cast off our red shirts and our aprons, and dressed ourselves like ladies and gentlemen at home to sit down to our meal, I was reminded of children playing at a feast, the girls having prepared it, while the boys painted their little boat.

Tuesday, June 9. The bride was in church, and as she wore white gloves, I suppose it was considered a formal appearance, though most informal it appeared, as she sat on one bench and her husband several benches behind her. She was dressed in a rich drab silk, with fancy straw, or chip bonnet, and white ribbons.

[1] Mrs. Wallis.

On Sunday we sat up very late, listening to and talking over all the news John had picked up during his visit to Peterboro and since. Another love affair has been confided to him by one of our circle. It is to end in nothing, but there is one feature in the case so novel and so droll that I must tell it you. The lady, though afterwards more distinct in her refusal, at first replied to congratulations that she was engaged to her suitor until the first of October, and though she should certainly never marry the gentleman, yet that before that date she could not consider herself at liberty to form any other engagement. It was more than a week afterwards that the gentlemen further ascertained her determination also not to marry himself. On Monday we received John's instructions respecting garden, etc., and made preparation for the departure, making out a list of errands for him at Toronto. John started this afternoon in his canoe. When the time came he looked as if he did not half like leaving his concerns here, but I hope they will go on smoothly. The chief business on hand at present is happily under Taylor's inspection, being the drains and foundations of the new building, erecting the fence, preparing lime, etc.

Wednesday, June 10. This morning we thought we were going to have visitors to breakfast. A boat was at the landing with a parasol in it. It was Mr. and Mrs. Hoare going a trip down the lake, and they left word that they would call as they came back, and take a cup of tea with us, which they accordingly did. This is the first time my mother has seen the lady, and she pronounces her a good sort of woman, which is just the description I should give of her. I am glad to see that she seems much more happy and cheerful than she used to be. We had many discussions on topics connected with women's duties in this country,— the management of a dairy, etc. I think it very likely that we may get a useful hint or two from her experience. She makes her butter in the Devonshire fashion, and I think in winter it may be an improvement upon our own way, for we are sadly plagued with the cream getting a bitter taste, which many consider is in consequence of cold. Perhaps the scalding may make it keep better. The various methods of making bread, cheese, candles, etc., were also commented upon, so you see what ladies talk about here. These useful topics are, however, not unmingled with a little general gossip.

Thursday, June 11. This day did not bring our expected visitors, Mr. and Mrs. Wallis, but another party, Mr. and Mrs. Fidler and their four young ones. All our visitors seem coming at once. These and those of yesterday, I fancy, have been waiting for the same event to set them at liberty—the launching of Mr. Hoare's boat. This is a new craft on the lake. There used to be so few that there was little difficulty in naming any that passed, but it is very different now. Mr. and Mrs. Wallis went down the lake a little after eleven, and passed here on their return between eight and nine, so I think they have returned the Dunsfords' visit fully—in length. We are a little dismayed to-night by finding that Taylor, our carpenter, is going home again, and that the new building must pause for a week or ten days. He has a house to build for himself this summer, besides his crops to look after.

Friday, June 12. A cool, cloudy morning sent us all a-weeding into the garden. John would not have been well pleased to see some of us at work, but so long as anything wants doing it is very difficult, and for my mother perfectly impossible, to keep quiet, so there can be no quiet for her in this country. We tried to get some of the children to weed, but none can be spared, everybody is planting potatoes. Our kitchen garden being new ground requires a great deal of attention in this respect. People can never increase their comforts without at the same time adding to their cares. The rain sent us in, and I got a little more work out of my needle than I often do. One ought to get all one's sewing done in winter, for though gardening is by no means a regular occupation now, yet, one way or other, time slips away most sadly at this season. We have a subject of anxiety at present which, as peculiar to this country, I must relate.

The horses are wandering somewhere in the bush, and day after day a man is employed in hunting for them, but they do not turn up. You know some of the *contre-temps* of last winter, how old "Rattler" died, and when a successor was provided the roads suddenly failed, and the horses were almost useless. When Mr. Toker[1] went to England John agreed to take his horses during his absence, in order that he might keep two ploughs going, also providing himself with a new plough. This, on the first day's using, broke, and though it could easily be repaired by the blacksmith, yet none other could do it, and our Vulcan had the day before met with a severe accident. So John's plans were frustrated, yet he had his two pair of horses to keep. He is not well off for pasture this year, and a little time since, as is a common practice here, he turned his own pair out into the bush, taking them by water to Sturgeon Point, that they might not come straight home. Now that it is time to look after them the search seems more difficult than we expected, and though the men seem to think it impossible they can be lost, their prolonged absence makes one very uneasy.

Sunday, June 14. The bride [Mrs. Wallis] looked much better than on the Sunday of her first appearance. Her dress was of another shade, richer than the former. I think it would have stood erect by itself. From John's observations last Sunday, and my mother's to-day, I find I look somewhat too simply dressed and unfashionable amongst them. I have no objection to improve in the latter respect as I wear out my present stock and get more knowledge of what ought to be. But if I can keep a resolution I will not improve in the former. If the follies and extravagances of the world are to be introduced upon Sturgeon Lake, we might as well, I think, move on to Galt Lake. I am afraid women deteriorate in this country more than the other sex. As long as the lady is necessarily the most active member of her household she

[1] Mr. Toker's daughter married a son of Mr. Dunsford. He owned the land around Red Rock, according to his granddaughters, the Misses Dunsford of Lindsay.

keeps her ground from her utility; but when the state of semi-civilisation arrives, and the delicacies of her table, and the elegancies of her person become her chief concern and pride, then she must fall, and must be contented to be looked upon as belonging merely to the decorative department of the establishment and valued accordingly. We are glad to have the Major's counsel respecting the stray horses. Though we had three men in the woods to-day (being the only day on which there was a chance of mustering so many), and their visible tracks were seen, yet these men came home at an early hour without them.

My mother is tired to-night, not altogether with her bodily exertions, but in part with talking and listening more than usual. She heard Mr. Fidler much better than she expected, and was much pleased with his sermon. Though an advocate of good dressing she does not defend a wreath of tiny roses ornamenting the inside of Mrs. Fidler's white-silk bonnet. She thought that I looked much more like the parson's wife. Poor Miss Fidler was a contrast to her pretty step-mother, being very homely and forlorn in her appearance. I warned you I should write a womanish journal!

Tuesday, June 16. In the afternoon we had the great satisfaction of seeing the men return each with a horse. This reminded me of a sermon of Mr. Mayow's on the unsatisfying nature of earthly possessions, when he illustrated part of his subject by this very circumstance—"a man that has two horses is not therefore a happy man, but if he comes to lose them he is immediately an unhappy man."

The flower that has been contemplated with most delight this season was a little daisy, which has unaccountably found its way on to our grass plot. We had none of us seen one for years, and it was greeted by all, in parlour and kitchen, as an old friend.

Saturday, June 20. We had been wishing to go up to the Falls all this week for my mother to make her calls upon all the newcomers. Our boat was sufficiently staunch, but the winds were too high. This morning, after many deliberations, we decided to go. We took an early dinner, and started between two and three. We first walked up to Mr. Wallis's and there had the pleasure of dropping our cards for the first time since we came to the backwoods. Mr. and Mrs. Wallis had gone down to Peterboro early this morning, to remain away about a fortnight. Painting, etc., appears to be going forward, so the bride means to polish up the bachelor's mansion. When they return they will be accompanied by some of Mrs. Wallis's Kingston friends. After leaving Mr. Wallis's we called on Mrs. Fidler and Mrs. Hoare. Mr. Hoare[1] went for Mrs. Fidler to join us, and we spent a sociable afternoon, being in our boat again, I think, before six. Mr. Hoare took my mother into his garden, and Mrs. Hoare took my mother into her dairy, etc. We got a present of a cowslip. I mentioned our little daisy. Mrs. Fidler did not even know what a daisy was!

Extract from a letter from ANNE LANGTON *dated 14 August, 1840.*

To sit at an embroidery frame is a contrast to my frame of dip candles. Thank you for the information you got for me. Part of it will be useful, but the plan of dipping by means of a pulley is scarcely applicable to my small scale of operations. More frequently I have a very small quantity of tallow, so that a box to admit six or seven candles is all I can well afford, as I have no means of keeping up the temperature but by replenishing from the fire. A small stick with six candles on it can be dipped by the hand as easily as any other way. What I have gained from your enquiries is that I ought to raise them from the tallow more slowly than I have been accustomed to do.

From the journal of ANNE LANGTON, *September, 1840.*

Once more I have folded my large sheet to complete my series of journals. September opens with a busy household

[1] He was Mr. Jameson's father-in-law and with Mrs. Hoare occupied Jameson's former house at Fenelon Falls.

day, the details of which are commonplace and uninteresting, so I will devote the space allotted to it to telling you what we have recently been about. There have been two events since the departure of our last letter. The first an expedition to Balsam Lake, the party consisting of Mr. and Mrs. Wallis, Mr. Hamilton and his mother, John and I, and two Mr. Dundases, the one having a brother visiting him at present. We went in canoes, the rapids being practicable only for this craft. One of the objects of the expedition was a visit to Admiral Vansittart and his wife, now resident for the season on Balsam Lake, but this was unhappily frustrated by a thunderstorm, which occurred in the middle of the day, and detained us under cover of the woods until it was too late. The time however was not unpleasantly spent, the formation of a camp with canoes and blankets on poles, the fire-lighting and pot-boiling, all having novelty to recommend them. After consuming our prog very snugly, notwithstanding the storm, we were favoured with a beautiful afternoon, and enabled to ascend the rapids, and take a peep at the lake, though we could not proceed much further. The day was voted a very pleasant one, and we reached the Falls again about sunset, where John and I remained until the following morning.

Wednesday, September 2. I do not know whether it was the pleasure of the day at Balsam Lake or not that put it into the heads of people to wish for something similar again in another quarter, but a little picnic has been resolved upon for the tenth of this month to take place at Sturgeon Point, and a couple of boat races are to form the excuse for a meeting. But it is on no account to bear the name of a regatta.

Thursday, September 3. The event of the day has been the receipt of English letters. . . . A source of satisfaction in vour letter was the ten pounds for Fenelon Falls church, which comes most opportunely for the advancing of the parsonage, to which we feel no hesitation in applying it. The building has caused some unpleasant feelings lately, and harmony seemed to be impaired. Mr. Wallis, as resident, was to have been the acting trustee, but he has given himself too little trouble concerning it, the consequence being that Mr. Fidler has assumed too much the direction of the work-people. Mr. Wallis, too, appears to have been not sufficiently firm and explicit as to what could and what could not be done, and Mr. Fidler has indulged in some whims and extravagances, which have made the expenses run up much faster than they should have done. Now consequently, when the funds are exhausted, the house is still extremely incomplete. As it is manifestly in a great measure Mr. Fidler's fault that the sums subscribed and advanced have been insufficient to finish the building, it is only fair that he should bear the extra expense, especially as he enjoys from the Society and the trustees an income of £180 a year currency, and is as competent as almost any of his parishioners to disburse a little on the occasion. The ten pounds will be a great lift, and the unknown but suspected donor has our gratitude.

Sunday, September 6. We have now the pleasure of work-people both inside and outside the house. We have cleaned out a room or two for the plasterers. The painter is at work on our exterior, and we are greatly lamenting that we have not also our carpenter about us. The finishing of a house is an endless job in this country, where work goes on for a few days, and then sowing, or reaping, or logging, or some other farming operation puts a stop to it again for a time. . . . You may generally imagine me in an evening with my frame before me, as I am just now very straight with common making and mending. My needle being thus at liberty has induced me to commence my great undertaking[1]. . . . We had some Peterboro ladies at church (visitors of Mrs. Dennistoun's), who made it look very gay, and exhibited to us some, I should fancy, very extreme fashions. The Major returned with us to dinner.

[1] The seat and back of a chair.

September

Monday, September 7. As the garden formed a prominent topic of the last journal, you will like to hear it named again. There is little doing in it at present. The next operation, I suppose, will be the preparation of it for winter repose. Though it did not promise very well early in the year, it has afforded us an ample supply of some vegetables. We have a few most excellent melons, and one or two watermelons. Tomatoes are just ripening, but the curiosity of the garden is a vegetable-marrow plant, which occupies a very large portion of it, and if its shoots had been trained to extend, instead of bending inwardly again, it might pretty nearly have streched itself over the whole. The fruit upon it is abundant, but early frosts prevent much of it coming to perfection. What does reach perfection is of great size. One specimen, which we have been cutting at for nearly a week, weighed twenty pounds. It is, moreover, a very good kind, and one which will keep some time on into the winter.

Tuesday, September 8. This is the last day of the plasterers, and as usual the plot thickens as we advance. A hearthstone here, and a chimney there, requiring a touch of the trowel, have by degrees introduced them into nearly every room in the house.

Wednesday, September 9. A busy day. Some cooking preparations for to-morrow, and, moreover, putting the house to rights after a pair of as dirty plasterers as ever mixed mortar. A strong south wind, continuing to blow for the third day, promises but very ill for the weather to-morrow, the day of the picnic. However, a thunderstorm this evening may be perhaps the crisis, and we may yet have a fine day. John and Mr. Dundas have been at Sturgeon Point pitching the marquee, and we ladies have been doing our part by the following preparations: two roast fowls, two roast wild ducks, a chicken, a piece of ham, a cranberry tart, two moulds of boiled rice with cranberry jelly, a bun loaf, bread, melons, etc., all most beautifully packed in a tin box. The arrival of your first package at Whitby is announced to us to-day. We have also another piece of agreeable intelligence, —postage is at length reduced to us poor colonists by Halifax, the price of a letter will be about elevenpence halfpenny, and we may send one that way for twopence halfpenny.

Thursday, September 10. The sun shone very brightly upon us this morning. John started early, whilst I waited and was taken in by a boatful of ladies from Cameron's Lake. We went down, twelve of us, in a new six-oared boat of Mr. Wallis's; he and his wife are away at Toronto. The Fidlers did not come because they are on the move to the parsonage, and the Frasers failed because the lake was too rough for a very small boat. The rest of the lake-dwellers assembled, twenty-eight in number. The day went off well but not exactly as was intended. The races did not come off at all, some of the expected boats having failed to attend, and those attending not affording good matches. The *Alice* performed a *pas seul* for our amusement and beautifully she acquitted herself. When this sport was over another very important occupation commenced, namely that of spreading and consuming our repast. I shall not give you the contents of the other prog baskets, as I did of our own, suffice it to say that there was a plentiful supply of all our backwoods delicacies, which were duly enjoyed. Meanwhile there had been two or three showers, and we thought of finishing with a dance under the marquee, John being equal to a set of quadrilles on the bugle; but the accumulation of thick clouds led Mrs. Hamilton to be anxious to return, so the party began to disperse, and I was housed long before sunset. I thought the day a very pleasant one.

Sunday, September 13. Mary went over the lake to see her friends, so we were quite without domestics. . . . Whilst managing the kitchen fire I had a meditation on the perversity of human nature. In England the servants are always crying out for chips. Here they accumulate in the wood-yard to a most inconvenient extent, and you cannot get the servants to make use of them. They are good solid chips that are made in chopping, and they make a most beautiful fire. Though they do burn away fast, yet a large boxful may be gathered in five minutes from the little mountain of them that rises under the axe. But as long as there is a pile of cut wood they burn it by the armfulls, without any help from the beautiful store of chips, which have to be carted away from time to time. Last year we burnt it where it stood, but the fire was scarcely quite extinguished in a month's time, and required constant watchfulness. Often, if there was a little wind, a bucket of water had to be carried out at night to prevent the embers kindling up again. An unusual incident has occurred this evening, which I must record. An enclosure with notes of invitation has been delivered to us. The Dunsfords ask us for the twenty-third, and to stay a few days. Part of the family will accept, and for part of the time.

Friday, September 18. I have looked over my wardrobe and fashionised a dinner-dress,—the first time I have wanted one since I wore colours. . . . We had another wedding announced to us yesterday—our neighbour Sally Jordan has given all her old lovers the slip, and is to be united on Monday to a young man who only came out this summer. We shall miss her very much. There is no other person near us who can come and lend us a helping hand on every occasion, so I cannot but lament the circumstance on our own account, and I have a good excuse for not rejoicing, as people say this match is made by her father and not by herself. This will be the second wedding at Fenelon Falls. There is a great assemblage of company at that celebrated place at present. The Wallises have a party in the house, the Fidlers likewise, and the people on Cameron's Lake have also company. I expect the church will scarcely hold us all on Sunday. I told you of the depredations here. I have just been in the kitchen, where I hear that Jordan had a six-months' old calf worried by wolves last night. I hope they will not fall in love with John's beautiful little bull, now about three months old.

Sunday, September 20. Yesterday we received the magnificent present of two hind-quarters of mutton from Jordan, and to-day came a few apples from Mr. Fidler. Last year we had a present of half a dozen from the same quarter. Things vary in value in different situations. These six were the only ones we saw during the season. We have an ague patient in the neighbourhood, the first since we came.

It is to be doubted whether the rising of the water, owing to the works at Bobcaygeon, will not render our lake less healthy. It spoils its beauty in many parts. The trees dying on the low ground near its margin, the pretty point which terminates our bay is greatly injured, and the landing for part of the year is very bad.

Monday, September 21. Mary was five hours in getting over the lake to us. She brought a boy with her whom, at any rate for a time, we shall engage. He is about the right age, and has a pleasant countenance, so perhaps he may suit us, which will be very well, as it is high time we should be provided with a wood-chopper.... The day has been a busy one. We have cleared out the drawing-room for the painter, having resolved to finish off this one room. The bookcases and other wood-work are to be light oak, which will have very much the same hue that we have been accustomed to, as pine after two or three winters' smoke is not very white. We have purchased a quarter of beef to-day, so there is work cut out for to-morrow.

Tuesday, September 22. Another busy day. Besides the disposal of our beef there was tomato ketchup to make, and melons to perserve, by way of making the most of the last fruits of this year's gardening. We weighed up vegetable marrow from one plant to 207 lbs., besides some that were left and spoiled, and another plant has produced upwards of 100 lbs. weight.

Friday, September 25. We had a beautiful day on Wednesday, and a pleasant sail down the lake to Mr. Dunsford's. This was the first time I had been to the house. It is a very good one, proportioned in all its dimensions to the size of the family, and the situation of it is about the best on the lake. A slight sketch I have taken, which you will get some day or another, will give you some idea of that end of the lake, which is decidedly superior to ours. Our party was to have been more numerous, but they had had disappointments, and it consisted only of our two selves, and three or four of the gentlemen of that end of the lake. However, the family party alone is so large that with only these few additions to it we mustered a very good dance in the evening. The quadrilles were varied by songs, duets on the harp and piano, etc.

Thursday was a brilliant day, and it was proposed that we should go down to Bobcaygeon, of which I was very glad. It is decidedly the most picturesque spot on the lakes, but its wood and water are not easily represented. They should have more skilful treatment than mine. However I made one or two slight attempts. Mr. Need gave us a little luncheon on the rocks. He has been building himself a house this summer, which has been named by someone or other the Lady-trap, greatly to Mrs. Dunsford's horror, who cannot see it as a joke, but thinks it quite shocking!

The second evening passed much as the first—a little more music, and a little less dancing—and we departed soon after breakfast this morning.

In a letter dated October 24 the arrival of the package number two early in the month is announced. . . . The presents of carpets, hearth-rugs, cord and twine are mentioned as specially acceptable. The writer says:

The wood fires make sad work with hearth-rugs, and indeed the burning goes beyond them, notwithstanding our fenders. Mr. Wallis said last winter that he found all his table cloths were full of holes from the wood flying. Our dinner-table has not quite escaped, though I fancy placed more distant from the fire than his had been. The servants here are reckless about wood. They are accustomed in their own shanties to one large room, with a chimney of immense dimensions, which they fill with logs. Our carpenter described his usual fire in winter to consist of the back log, a foot in diameter, and one upon that little less in size, and three others in front, with some split pieces. The quantity of wood we consume is ruinous, and it is often inconvenient to John to spare the men to bring it up. We shall now be very soon making up our winter pile. . . .

The new room is finished, all but putting in the furniture. It will be a relief not to have to vacate our rooms for our guests.

We are not quite ready for winter yet. Some of our fences are yet incomplete, and John is putting up a new building—a workshop, a most desirable addition to the premises. Our present joiner's shop would not do for that purpose, as it would prevent our claiming the benefit of the insurance in case of any accident. Such a building must be, according to regulation, at least 66 ft. from the house and out-buildings. Ours will be about 80 ft. It is immediately behind the house, but unfortunately, from the great rise in the ground, must be conspicuous. It is to be of dimensions that will allow of boats, carts, etc., being manufactured or repaired in it, and will enable men to be profitably occupied in wet weather. Our new room is finished, but we have had so many hindrances lately that it is not yet furnished.

I do not know whether we told you that these townships have been recently embodied into a militia regiment, of which Mr. Fraser is Colonel and Mr. Wallis Major. John is one of the Captains. He mustered his Company the other day for the first time, but only to collect their subscriptions towards the re-erection of General Brock's monument at Queenston. A rate according to rank was to be asked, but not required, of all militia men. John's party came forward very readily—I think they are thirty-six in number. Mr. Hamilton is his lieutenant, and he has some old soldiers for his subordinate officers. Some of John's commissions will concern his costume *à la militaire*, as the officers are expected to have the undress uniform. We shall send our orders early, that the things may come by the first spring ships—otherwise they are thrown too late in the season.

Extract from letter from JOHN LANGTON *to* WILLIAM LANGTON *dated 30 November, 1840.*

Your packages I have no doubt the ladies will have told you have arrived with no great damage, but I have some doubts whether they have told you anything of what damage has occured for my mother seems to think it an offence little short of high treason to find fault with anything you do. Now I am prepared to allow that you may be a good Christian, son, brother, husband, father, and banker to boot, without being quite faultless as a packer; and therefore I will humbly suggest a few rules for your future guidance in that particular. First, packages intended to be shifted about from one conveyance to another, and to be transported in boats especially, should not exceed a hundredweight each, which those two nearly doubled. Smaller packages are more handy to move about, and the contents likewise receive less damage. Secondly, when there are a multitude of things to be put into several boxes they should be classed; thus heavy articles should be kept as much together as possible and not be mixed with fragile ones; articles which if injured by carriage are likely to injure other things should be kept separately likewise, and the light and easily damaged articles should have their separate place. This should be observed not only in the arrangement of the larger packages but also in the smaller ones which compose the larger. Thus the barrel is a heavy affair and should not have formed part of the miscellaneous cargo, both because from its weight it must have grievously crushed the sago etc., when in the many turns and reverses of this world it happened to be uppermost, and likewise because it might have leaked and steeped the said sago prematurely. Thus also the preserves might have gone very well with the flower-pots and bottles, neither could have much damaged the other and in weight they were pretty much on a par. But books and merino gowns should have been kept apart from such dangerous neighbours. Thus also a lamp glass delicately packed in paper shavings should not have been accompanied by two ponderous rouleaus of shillings, which to judge from appearances must, like the bull in the china shop, have had fine times of it on the passage! Thirdly, as to the materials in which things are packed I beg to submit that brown paper, though when close pressed between two other substances as between the side of a vessel and the copper sheeting it turns water very well, is not *per se* waterproof, and that if a jar of preserves with a paper cover is turned upside down, the paper allows the syrup to escape, leaving a residue of black currants which would make, I daresay, an excellent addition to a bun loaf. Moreover, when wet it is a very fragile article through which the currants themselves even can escape. The consequence of this has been that the Reviews will be very hard reading, though sweet, for the leaves are most obstinately glued together with black currant syrup: fortunately, however, the damage among the books is exclusively confined to Reviews and magazines, though a strong smell of mixed syrup and vinegar pervades the whole contents of the box. From the same fragility of brown paper the sago was evenly and most intimately distributed throughout the whole substance of box no. 1 with the exception perhaps of the interior of the barrel. Sir Sam Romilly alone upon inspection was found to contain at least a teacupful of sago and, for a fortnight after, I kept finding grains of sago in my pockets and shoes and in everything about the house; some of the flower-pots had parted with their earth and in its place we found sago. Paper will do very well for solid or for light things like tea, but sago is too heavy for it. I must observe however one thing in favour of brown paper which I have so much calumniated, viz. that books, merino and sundry other things wrapped in paper were perfectly uninjured though rather damp, even when the paper was so completely soaked with syrup that one could not unwrap the parcel without the paper coming to pieces in one's hands. Preserves should have bladder over the top, or, what I have found more perfect still, should be put in jars narrow enough in the neck to be closed with a cork. I should also recommend that, if it is necessary to put an article like preserves which damage other things together with articles susceptible of damage, the preserves might be put in a tin case or a box surrounded with four or five folds of brown paper whereby their leakage, if any, might be kept to themselves. Do not imagine from this dissertation that there has been much injury; little else has suffered except the lamp-glass and the Reviews and preserves, the one by absorption, the other by depletion. As for the sago it is a clean article and its *disjecta membra* have been collected without much loss. Only one of the bottles (vinegar) was broken. I have dissertated so far principally because more damage may occur again from the same causes.

ANNE LANGTON *writes*:

I have left myself but a few minutes to finish the sheet, but the week will soon be recorded. John made as expeditious a journey to Peterboro as he could, any day might have closed the water communication. He had most miserable weather but was none the worse for it. Since his return we had a visit of a couple of days from Edward Atthill previous to departure. The new workshop raised its lofty head yesterday; it will not be an embellishment to the place but I hope will make up for that in usefulness.

I am sorry to say that we have got Mary an invalid again. She is a most melancholy patient and I begin to think will scarcely be able to keep her place this winter. At present Mrs. Woods (Sally Jordan that was) is again our help in need. She lives at her father's this winter but the future plans of the young couple are not decided.

My mother thinks John has been rather too strong on the subject of packing but some of his hints will be useful ones. We certainly never think we have said enough to give you an idea how much pleasure these packages afford, and how much we feel your debtors for the execution of our numerous commissions and for the presents you add to them. The hearth-rugs are quite beautiful and the carpet will make our new room perfect.

1841

Extracts from a letter from Anne Langton *dated 1 January, 1841.*

We have been putting the finishing stroke to our new room. It is spacious, commodious, and cheerful-looking. The house is certainly now a very warm one; our room is a totally different thing to what it was before the house was plastered. Our Christmas Day party is now greatly reduced. The married men, of course, no longer belong to it, and Mr. Dennistoun entertains his own clan, which includes all Cameron Lake. Mr. Need, Mr. Boyd, Mr. Jones, and Mr. McLaren were our guests. On Christmas Day we had a card table, a backgammon table, and a chess table,—the first time I have played chess since I came out. There are a few things still to do for the house. The chief one is the manufacture of an icehouse, a most desirable thing in this country, as it is the only chance of having occasionally fresh meat in summer-time. At this season we are well supplied, and we have lately been laying in summer supplies. Besides pork barrels we have now six sides of bacon and thirteen hams decorating our kitchen ceiling.

It is an easy transition from the housekeeping to the household, and that most important of all topics here— the domestics. We have at present a young woman who has lived with two or three different families in this neighbourhood, and has the character of being an "excellent servant" which means here one that will do your bidding. Our other servant is a boy of about thirteen, decidedly very clever. He has learnt his house duties very well, and at present always waits at table. He keeps us very well supplied with wood too, and looks very properly after his pigs and poultry. Moreover, he is very civil and obliging in manner, and therefore suits us very well. I hope he may continue to do so. The new work-shop at the top of the hill is now finished, and, contrary to our expectation, is no eye-sore, but rather the contrary, as it is a most respectable building, and adds importance to the appearance of the place. The flag-staff now surmounts it instead of decorating the house. The old joiner's shop we purpose converting into a room for John, and making the room above it his bed-room. His old house is getting very crazy and cold, and he will be glad to make the change before next winter. His bachelor visitors will be as easily accommodated there as in his present dwelling.

From the journal of ANNE LANGTON *for February, 1841.*

Monday, February 1. If I begin to tell you any of the day's transactions, I shall weary you with repetition, their very counterparts having often been recorded before, all I think but the ruling of account books this evening, for the use of the present year.

I was rather weary of adding, subtracting, and multiplying this morning. Being just about to lose three of my eldest scholars, I am trying to drive as much into them as I can. When they are gone I shall take my other big one only once a week, leaving one day for infant schooling. I have one or two who stick fast at their letters, and will be the better for some more particular drilling.

Tuesday, February 2. I boasted rather too soon in one of my letters of our stock of seasoned firewood, for very shortly after we came to an end of it. One feels the change a good deal at first, for the management of a fire is so different with seasoned and unseasoned wood. There is a delightful glow from the embers after the wood is consumed, but if you let the fire get into that state, which after using dry wood one is very apt to do, a wet log or two, probably also caked with frozen snow, will put the embers out before they have time to kindle. You ought to replenish just when the fire is at its hottest, and the habit of doing so is I fancy what has caused such ruinous extravagance in the use of our dry wood.

Wednesday, February 3. My small school effort here flourishes, whereas Mr. Fidler's school at Fenelon fell off gradually in numbers, and now is no more.

Thursday, February 4. Margaret kindly offers to choose a bonnet for me. I fashioned a little the green velvet one I had in England, which is quite good, and made it look, I think, very nice, but I have only once put it on, for my little fur cap is so much warmer, and my mother saying it is becoming also I have overcome the reluctance I felt at first to sit at church without the shade of a bonnet. My summer headgear does not sound well in the description, as my choice lay between a bonnet of my mother's and one of my aunt's, the latter taking one of my mother's in exchange. My mother's drawn brown-silk bonnet, somewhat altered to suit me, really is very pretty, and Aunt Alice's large poke leghorn very snug and shady for a boat, and they are both in excellent preservation. There is this difference between our dress here and at home, that though a good and handsome thing is as becoming and appropriate at times here as with you, the occasions for wearing them are so very much fewer that they last for ever, and it is quite vain to attempt, without the most wasteful extravagance, to be always just in the fashion. Nothing wears out fast of the visible garments but shoes, stockings, and the printed gowns we wear in a morning, and which I always make in a fashion that allows me to dispense with collars. This enables me to be neat with much less time and trouble. These dresses get pretty hard usage, as recorded in a previous page, but I always consider myself perfectly presentable in them during any of the morning hours, and in summer until tea-time.

Mr. Wallis' marriage has been an acquisition to us indirectly, by setting his married housekeeper at liberty, who was a dressmaker by profession. I am trying her skill at present. I must not expect that she will fit me as well as I have learnt to fit myself, but it is a relief not to have a dress to make in short and busy days.

Sunday, February 7. To give you an idea of the brightness of our snow-clad world, I may tell you that last night, although it was so much overcast that I could not distinguish where the moon was, yet did I see without a light that the thermometer was at 27. I have one very interesting circumstance to mention—I put the finishing stitch to the centre-piece of my chair, namely, the coat-of-arms. I did not accompany John to church this morning. He took a large packet of despatches for the post. The Eldon men of his militia Company seem to have excited his admiration. They are all Highlanders, and, he says, "a magnificent set of fellows." We had an excellent apple-tart to-day, made of dried apples, quartered and strung on threads, as we used to see them in Italy. When used you soak them well first, then boil them in the same water, and crush them in their own juice, sweeten and put into your tart. A bag of these is a most convenient store.

Tuesday, February 9. Mr. Boyd, it is suspected, will one day be an aspirer to the hand of Miss Caroline Dunsford.

Wednesday, February 10. My mother and aunt have been baking gingerbread, whilst I made a slight alteration in my new dress. I am happy to say that the dressmaker has performed admirably, and I shall have no hesitation in trusting her another time.

Thursday, February 11. I understand that Mr. Fidler intends to recommence schooling in his own house. He did teach in the church, and I can fancy that having to meet his scholars there, and to have a fire lighted, would make an irregular attendance much more annoying.

Friday, February 12. We had a great biscuit-making to-day, and the very unusual interruption of a party of callers, Mr. and Mrs. Dunsford, with their eldest son and daughter, about the first time that Mr. Dunsford had been out of doors this winter, and a very cold day they selected for their drive. They came along the new road, which, for want of more travelling upon it, is indifferent, but it promises to be a good one in time. It is curious that seldom as we see this family, a visit either to or from them should happen to figure in most of my journals. Mr. Dunsford says his novel is the most delightful amusement to him.[1] He is very ready to talk about it, so that the fact of there being one in progress is spoken of, I hear, at a great distance from Sturgeon Lake.

Monday, February 15. Mr. Fidler had engaged John and me to dine with them on Saturday. Mr. Dundas, his brother, and Mr. McLaren were the only other guests, and the evening was a quiet and pleasant one. The parsonage felt warm and comfortable. They patronise stoves altogether, and the method of warming the upper rooms is by carrying the stove-pipes from below through them, having one or two turnings in them to increase the effect. This plan must answer very well, for the previous cold night was the first on which any ice had been seen in a room so warmed. The upper story of the parsonage is not nicely planned, having been divided into too many small apartments, but below the rooms are good. Mr. Fidler complains that now one and then another takes him to task, sometimes for beginning the service too soon, and sometimes too late. Each one would have his own watch regulate the parish. John is very busy manufacturing a dial for him out of the slates you sent out.

Tuesday, February 16. A large party of young men have assembled at John's cottage to-night to start together for

[1] The novel eventually appeared in the Peterborough newspaper and was entitled *The King's Messengers.*

Peterboro in the morning, but they have declined joining us at tea, being, I suppose, in travelling costume. I daresay that John's expedition will warm him a little on the subject of the coming election, the universal topic, I understand, everywhere, but here we are mighty indifferent. I suppose that Mr. Bolton, our guest of last summer, will have John's vote, if he gives it at all. One of the candidates bears a most despicable character, and yet, though admitted by all to be everything that is bad, little short of, if not actually a murderer, many suppose that he will get in. I hope, for the honour of the Province, not; but, unfortunately, a vast number of the small farmers are in his debt, and he threatens to sue them unless they give him their votes, and influence their relatives to do the same.

Wednesday, February 17. We have had an exceedingly dirty job this afternoon. We lighted the stove in our spare room in order to thaw the snow out of the pipe, but it would not draw at all, and after sundry experiments with the damper, we were obliged to take the fire out, the pipe down, disjoint it, and, what was far more difficult, put it together again and in its place. However, our perseverance was rewarded, for we discovered and remedied the evil. Our boy, Timothy, is a clever little lad, with twice the head that most of them have.

Thursday, February 18. I have been disappointed to-day. I had intended having only a small school for a time, and promised myself great improvement in some of my little dull ones, when they would have more exclusive attention bestowed upon them. But I have a message of application already from the successors to Daniel's farm, who have a family of children, and I suppose next week I shall receive all those who are above six years old and know their letters.

Friday, February 19. There will have been another disappointment to-day, I am afraid, not to us, but to a poor man and woman who have heard in Ops reports of my mother's medical skill, and had come to consult her. The woman, for a disease of two years' standing, got a few rhubarb pills; and the man, for a complaint in his leg, a bit of flannel. They brought likewise the case of a third person before us, for whom they got nothing, for we dare not prescribe.

Mrs. Russell asks leave to go and see her children again, and gives a most exceedingly broad hint that she wants something good to take with her, so she is to go to-morrow, and have a cake for them.

Saturday, February 20. Our ducks did not do well this winter. We lost them both. They bear cold very ill. The other birds are well and fat, and we have had a few eggs from time to time all winter. "Robin," the horse, is pronounced well again, but he has had a long confinement, and I am afraid will not have earned his oats this winter.

Sunday, February 21. A thaw day and a bright sun brought torrents of water down where the new and old roofs join. John thinks it will be difficult to make it secure, but Taylor expects that he can manage it, though he has not succeeded yet.

Hard frost is very inconvenient in one's larder. You cannot lay by a little broth or gravy without its becoming as hard as a stone, sometimes breaking the vessel that contains it, and not available on short notice. Just now we are specially inconvenienced, for we cannot get into our larder by any means. I do not say that this is exactly from the frost, but it is owing to variations in the atmosphere, acting upon imperfectly seasoned wood, now shrinking it, now swelling it, and destroying the perpendicularity of the door-posts, so that the doors not infrequently will refuse to shut or open. In the present case I suppose we shall have to use force at last.

Monday, February 22. I am to have two new scholars on Thursday, a boy of Powell's, our new neighbour, and one of Jordan's, the latter I daresay fourteen or fifteen years old. My mother is going to superintend the sewing department. Aunt Alice thinks that I have been very negligent to give so little attention to this important branch of education; but really, without undervaluing it, I have found since I had so many scholars that I had no time to fix work. Two days a week is not sufficient for everything, and I consider that the mothers will teach a little sewing because they derive immediate advantage from it, but with book learning it is otherwise.

Wednesday, February 24. Taylor came up this evening for the remainder of the cash due him, which he declined receiving at Christmas. His arrival was opportune for the opening of the larder door. It seems that it is the frost heaving up the ground that occasions many difficulties of this kind. Taylor has just been establishing a Sunday School at Bobcaygeon. He had been accustomed to teach in one at home, and, being a bit of a musician too, he can teach the children to sing hymns. Mr. Need also gives his assistance.

Sunday, February 28. Mr. and Mrs. Fidler called yesterday, and Mr. Fidler took away with him a very neat dial that John had constructed. Speaking of time, my little watch has performed very well since it came out again. Before that I wore the one you sent John (a most excellent one), when I was the great authority in the country, and my character for accuracy became quite established. The old timepiece, against all expectations, goes very well, and it is of great consequence to my mother.

Extract from a letter from ANNE LANGTON *dated 9 March, 1841.*

I am promised three or four scholars this week, one of my present children having made that announcement to me; but I have received no formal application, and I suspect that that ceremony is not thought at all requisite. Another family of children will be fixed near us in the course of the summer, and we shall presently have a pretty population within three miles of us. There is just now the incident of a wedding. A brother of John's man, William Ellis, had a young girl recommended to him the other day. He went down to see her, approved, proposed, and returned an engaged man. Last week he became a married man. There is expedition for you! He is a good steady workman, and if his choice is as good as prompt there will be another pair of respectable neighbours for us. Our stock of firewood is being drawn in by oxen, and a comfortable-looking pile of it is already in view of the kitchen window. Just now John has got a dial mania, and is manufacturing a miniature one to go upon a magnetic needle, the face of which will be silver, if a piece of money can be beaten out and carved light enough to turn. We selected one from the old coin collection, which I had not seen for many a day.

Extract from a letter from ANNE LANGTON *dated 8 April, 1841.*

We have been more fortunate with our poultry than any one of our neighbours. At the Falls weasels have been most destructive. We have seen none here except one, a beautiful white one, which I hope has left no progeny. This winter we have fed our poultry on grain. It may be rather expensive keep, but we had eggs during the winter, and now abundance of them. The election for the county has taken place, but the candidate for whom all our young men voted did not succeed in obtaining his election. John had to walk seventy or eighty miles to give his vote, sleeping where he could, and returned half famished and very much fatigued.

From the journal of ANNE LANGTON *for May, 1841.*

Sunday, May 2. We accomplished our long-talked-of visit to Mr. Dennistoun on April 12, Easter Monday, ice travelling being beautiful, and, indeed, the sleighing was still pretty good on much of the road, though the mud-holes were deepening and widening. John, who has had an annual upset hitherto, thought to escape this season, but he was mistaken. In rising out of one of these same mud-holes we went over; hovering for a few seconds over the black place, we just cleared it in time to have a more comfortable tumble. The day after we drove down the lake to call on the Frasers and Dunsfords. The ice was beautiful—the cutter almost went of itself. At this time there was small prospect of the lake opening soon. It was generally expected that May would be far advanced before we should have water communication. However, the last week of April, part of which was very hot, and part very windy, removed the ice from our prospect.... It has been a terrible season for the cattle. Many in the country have died—none of John's I am happy to say, but after having, some weeks ago, churned about three pounds of butter a week, we could for a time scarcely allow ourselves milk for our tea.

Monday, May 3. We had a numerous school this afternoon—ten. I have had a very poor attendance for some weeks, often only two dreadfully stupid ones, and one little one. This sudden increase has called for my mother's assistance in the sewing department, and also Aunt Alice's in hearing A B C, but I think I shall now be able to form something like a class. This can only be if they are pretty regular in their attendance, however. There are too many beginners now, with whom regularity is of importance, for me to indulge in a summer holiday, as last year. Some of my pupils, I doubt not, receive good religious instruction at home, but I fear others do not.

Friday, May 7. The lake was covered with fragments of ice this morning, brought down the river from Cameron's Lake. I fancy this is about the last of it.

Monday, May 10. Our housecleaning operations are interrupted. Our servant has had a letter requiring her presence about her own place. Mrs. Russell, our late servant, has been summoned to our assistance during her absence, and meanwhile, we have transferred our labours to John's house. My mother and I were very busy there all this morning, dismantling it, that the walls may be washed with scalding lye, a most desirable thing occasionally in sunbaked log-houses, to keep them clear of insects. We have had the first nice spring rain to-day, which makes us look forward to a better supply of milk and butter. Of my ten scholars, half were absent this afternoon.

Thursday, May 13. Last night, just as we were preparing to retire, we were startled by a rap at the parlour door. It was John's man, announcing his return, accompanied by five or six other gentlemen, and some bread and meat were wanted. We despatched the requisite, and a pile of blankets to meet so large a demand on a cold night. The gentlemen departed again before our breakfast hour. . . . John was very busy whilst in Peterboro, taking measures to promote a public meeting on the subject of opening the navigation of these lakes and rivers. It is to be hoped that private animosity will be suspended on the 29th of this month, when unanimity will be essential to the furtherance of the cause in hand. It is thought that the Governor-General is not favourable to us.

Friday, May 14. We have had a soap-boiling, amongst other things, but I do not take the same interest in it that I do in candle-making. I wish you could just take a view of another operation going forward at present,—the clearing away of the accumulation of chips in the woodyard. If that were not done occasionally, we should soon have our house standing at the foot, instead of on the top, of a hill.

Sunday, May 16. Yesterday we rubbed, white-washed, plastered and gardened, and finally unpacked a cargo of goods from Peterboro. It was high time our stores should be replenished. John recommends me to order a sidesaddle and habit, that he may mount me on Robin's back when the state of our navigation is not favourable. It certainly might be convenient at times; for instance, I should have gone to church to-day, which I did not. The lake looked black and rough, and our shipping is not yet in perfect order. John was wishing to-day that he could be split into two or three, there are so many things to attend to just at this season, things that cannot be committed to other hands. You must know there are a great many more hands than heads in this country, perhaps in every country.

Tuesday, May 18. John walked down to Bobcaygeon to-day, to concoct with Mr. Need resolutions for the meeting of the 29th. Not that this duty devolved upon them, but they thought it quite necessary that something of the sort should be prepared in case the committee appointed had never been able to agree. I daresay he will contrive to combine a visit to the Beehive with this important business. The readings of the novel are concluded, and I rather think music and flirtation will be quite as agreeable.

Thursday, May 20. John was at home this morning before we were down to breakfast. He brought with him some wild vines and other additions to our beauties . . . and is at this moment making up packets of flower-seeds for the Dunsfords. He has got a reinforcement in Mr. Dunsford to the University Club.[1] If they increase in numbers there may be some satisfaction in such a society, but at present it consists only of five or six. I had an application to-day to take another scholar, but I find it quite impossible to increase my numbers. I shall however make room for the applicant soon by dismissing one who has had the benefit of more than two years' teaching, and, I am sorry to say, to but little purpose. I begin to wish we had, or could have, something more regular in the way of a school. The number of children is increasing, and my cares are much more likely to increase than to decrease. Aunt Alice teaches a little every evening; our boy, Timothy, is her pupil—not a remarkably bright one, I am afraid.

Sunday, May 23. There have been several changes since

[1] A club of young men who had graduated at one of the two Universities, Oxford or Cambridge, soon abandoned.

I have been at church. The churchyard is fenced round,— it takes in all the hill,—the road changed, and the church fitted up with pews. This was decided upon by a majority at the Easter meeting. John formed the minority. Whether the advantages or disadvantages will be more remains to be seen. The pews are left without doors, to obviate exclusiveness, but as some of them are paid for by individuals, there will be some appropriation of them, and this in so small a place is undesirable.

Wednesday, May 26. We had a letter from a firm in Montreal, announcing the arrival of a barrel of biscuits, which, in consequence of its not being accompanied by an invoice, could not be forwarded. John doubts whether any invoice sent out after the knowledge of this omission is made known to you would be in time to prevent its being disposed of by auction, as the duty upon it cannot be determined; however, it might be as well to attempt to save it.

Thursday, May 27. John paddled up to the Falls this afternoon, and after tea set out for a moonlight walk down to Mr. Boyd's, from whence he joins a party in Mr. Dunsford's boat to proceed to-morrow to Peterboro. Of course most of the gentlemen on these lakes attend the meeting. I trust it will have a prosperous issue. Lord Sydenham, I understand, does not patronize water communication, expecting railways to supersede everything; and of course our particular claim to be the line of road only rests in our beautiful string of lakes and rivers.

Saturday, May 29. To-day I intend taking all the hams and the bacon down, and inspecting their condition. This is an operation that must be very frequently performed. There is a little beetle in this country that I had rather get rid of than even mosquitoes or black flies. It infests all our provisions. We intend putting up a smoke-house soon, which is the best way of keeping hung meat—about once a forthnight smothering the little creatures. I shall send you a small sketch of our addition and improvements.

Extract from a letter from Anne Langton, *dated 21 June, 1841.*

The meeting concerning the opening of navigation at Peterboro went off very well, somewhat against expectation, and some good result appears to be hoped for, at least by the sanguine. John was accompanied on his return by a Mr. Forbes, who is making acquaintance with the backwoods. He remained here a few days, and was entertained in backwoods fashion by being set to work. John and he got the boats painted, which are now again at their anchorage, enlivening the bay.

In a letter dated 30 July, 1841, Anne Langton mentions her final decision to use a small legacy in the purchase of some land upon which to put up a small building for a schoolhouse, the requisite number of children being there to qualify them for the Government grant of ten pounds per annum. The number of children in the immediate neighbourhood made it important to provide some regular instruction. Two applications had been already received for the post of master, and the neighbours volunteered to give their services for the building.

From the journal of Anne Langton *for August, 1841.*

Monday, August 2. John's harvest would have begun to-day, I suppose, but William Ellis had a "Bee." This will, I fancy, be the last of the "Bees" until I call for one to build a schoolhouse. John's man, William Ellis, is going to live at his own place, and in his room will be one Henry Brandon, who has also a wife and child. We have our new little man to-day and shall have a new maiden to-morrow.

Tuesday, August 3. Superintending my new boy, and preparing for my new girl have been the most engrossing occupations of the day. Mrs. Menzies came with her six children to take leave this afternoon—as fine a family as I ever saw. John Menzies had called by himself a day or two before, having expressed great fears that he should cry. He just held out during the short interview, but was overtaken by a regular break-down at John's house. I felt strongly inclined to weep a little too, when I kissed his eldest little girl, who had been quite one of my favourite scholars. The children looked all quite happy, with their new clothes, their cake, their little presents, and the world before them, and were no doubt full of bright anticipation.

I believe John Menzies is bound for Kingston, as the focus of everything, but without any distinct plan of what he is to do. The cause of his leaving here is that he could not make his farming answer. In fact, his wife has been little of a help to him, and I fear that elsewhere he will find his difficulties as great. As his family grow up I hope these will lessen, but I am afraid that they may be yet worse off before they are better. This family has been so long connected with Blythe and its master that we feel much interested about them.

Wednesday, August 4. John had a great disappointment in finding a mistake in the shaping of his sail. He has generally been a very successful sail-maker, and this is an unaccountable and very provoking blunder. My mother and I spent all the afternoon in the garden, transplanting lettuces, tying up vines, etc.

Saturday, August 7. There have been many departures from Peterboro, among the rest Mr. Kirkpatrick who is moving to Kingston, and we hear that Mr. Wallis is to occupy his house at Peterboro this winter. Whether this means a final departure from the Falls we do not know. The Tokers have taken leave of Sturgeon Lake also.

Monday, August 9. We had a party from across the lake this evening to consult us respecting a cut finger. A poor little lad of about five years of age had been handling an axe, and had almost severed the finger at the joint. Two days ago we were asked for sticking-plaster for a cut three inches long. This sort of accident is pretty frequent, and our store of court-plaster is dwindling very much. A further supply on the next opportunity will be very acceptable.

Tuesday, August 10. Venetian blind-making, sail-making, and stay-making have been my occupations this wet day, and my mother has been shoe-making, or rather covering a favourite pair of shoes the second time.

Wednesday, August 11. Servants here are, on the whole, not badly paid, but there is no scale of remuneration according to merit. You give a girl less than a woman but when they consider themselves women they must have four dollars a month. More than this you could not give them without exciting the wrath of all the housekeepers in the neighbourhood for raising wages. I believe it is the same as regards men, unless they have a trade. Knowledge and experience as farmers does not acquire for them additional recompense for their labour. The whole concatenation of circumstances that makes servants what they are in this country seems so natural to its present state that I am inclined to make the best of them, and expect nothing more. If there were skill to be had at a greater cost, there are so few that could afford to employ it that the supply would not be kept up. Girls never expect to remain long in service, and seldom do so long enough to gain much experience. They are too uncertain to be worth much teaching, at least it seems quite customary to leave them untaught. John visited in Port Hope last winter, where the dinner and wines were of the best, and the horses and sleighs of the handsomest, yet the lady of the house always laid the table herself. My mother said to one of our servants, "I shall iron that best tablecloth myself; I always do." "Indeed, ma'am," said the girl, "I think every lady irons her own best table linen." I am not more disposed to wonder at the deficiencies of our domestics than I am greatly to commend the honesty of the backwoods, where there are so few temptations, and fewer opportunities for dishonesty.

Sunday, August 15. It is four years to-day since we

landed at this place. There have been many changes and one grievous one since that time, but when I dwell upon my former period sufficiently long to bring it vividly before me with all its trials and anxieties, I generally find some cause for thankfulness, and so it is now.

Tuesday, August 17. I was much amused to-day with watching "Rock" and the cat. Puss had kittened this morning, and "Rock" takes the greatest interest in her young family. I found them by themselves in John's house, he sitting beside her, watching, and licking the kittens, and turning them over with his nose with the greatest delight and fondness, while she seemed highly pleased with his attentions.

Friday, August 20. I have been busy with my accounts, and neglected my journal for two days. Keeping accounts is a somewhat perplexing affair in this country of no cash. John, for instance, must keep an account open with almost half the population. He never goes to Peterboro without three or four neighbours coming with their little commissions, some bringing the money, and some not, some part of it, and so forth. Yesterday John and I went over to Cameron Lake to pay a visit to the Dennistouns, and fetch Margaret Hamilton. We had a beautiful day, and a pleasant breeze, and the *Fairy* performed admirably with her new sail. I had never seen Mr. Dennistoun's place except when the ground was covered with snow. We got home to tea, just before dark. You will not easily guess what had been my mother's occupation during our absence—manufacturing a pair of trousers for her new boy out of an old bed-tick. Nowhere but in this country would a lad have been sent out to service with such a scanty supply of rags. I am afraid that this second Timothy is too much of a child for us, requiring too much looking after. John has had a loss of four little pigs, carried away two successive nights by some wild beast,—most probably a bear. The bears are very fond of pork. He intends to sit up and watch to-night. Jordan had a three-months' old calf eaten by the wolves within his own clearing the other night.

Saturday, August 21. John kept watch all night, but saw nothing of the beast. However, two more pigs are missing, and these went in the daytime, and, moreover, were not very little ones.

We talked over the situation of the proposed school building. If we put it in the township of Fenelon, as desired, there will be required some chopping and burning before anything could be done, and as people are always pressed for time in this country, that may be a consideration. . . .

We had another application for sticking-plaster to-day, and two for medicine.

Tuesday, August 24. We have had applications for medicine again both yesterday and to-day, and our medicines are quickly disappearing. I am sorry to say that there is ague on the other side of the lake. We have yet seen nothing of it here. Our boy took it last spring, but it was after going for a day or two into Ops, which is a dreadfully unhealthy township.

Friday, August 27. John employed the wet day in completing a catalogue of the books, preparatory to the increase they are to have when the packages arrive. We muster amongst us about 1200 volumes.

The new School Act came into force for Verulam in November. The condition of the grant was the regular attendance of fifteen children, and the adoption of what was called the Irish system. Three trustees had to be appointed by the parents.

1842

In a letter, dated January 10, 1842, mention is made of John Langton having been appointed district councillor for Fenelon, under a new arrangement of Lord Sydenham's, whereby the interior business of each district was to be conducted within its own boundaries.

Mention is also made in the letter of January 9 that Mr. Need was returning to England, having inherited the fortune of an aunt. His departure was much regretted, as from his education and general information he was a most agreeable companion. The arrival in the colony is also noticed of Mr. Wickham, who afterwards became the husband of the eldest Miss Dunsford.

Extract from a letter from ANNE LANGTON *dated 3 February, 1842.*

Cord-wood is so called to distinguish it from logs or trees drawn in, often to be cut up at the door. A "cord" is a pile of pieces cut and split, four feet long, and the pile itself must be eight feet long and four feet high. These are cut again according to the length of the fireplaces, and often further split.

We have had Mr. Boyd with us for nearly a week, to keep quiet and nurse a cut foot. Since John left us he has come up to dine with us sometimes. He is a favourite of mine; he is not brilliant or animated, but has much goodness and kindness, and simplicity of character, and is an example to all our young men for industry, attention to business, and study of economy. He is about five- or six-and-twenty, and came out the year after John did.

The Fidlers have been with their friends at the Front. Poor Mrs. Fidler will have made sad complaints of the dullness of the backwoods; the situation is not in repute at present, and it is said that only English ladies can make themselves comfortable in such solitude. The Wallises are at Kingston now, and we had a call from Mr. Wallis a little time ago, when he came to look at his deserted place. He gave us an account of the splendours of the seat of government, the sledges and horses' trappings all new, to impress the mind of the newly-appointed governor, who, Mr. Wallis reports, is a fine-looking man, carrying his years with dignity. His ministers, on the contrary, seem to be a set of the shabbiest looking creatures, but many may have good heads for all that.

Extract from a letter from ANNE LANGTON *dated 3 March, 1842.*

Yesterday John attended the funeral of Henry Dunsford, who has been a great invalid both before and since arriving in this country. He was interred in their own grounds—a spot which Mr. Dunsford had selected soon after coming out for themselves and their family. Mr. Dunsford read the service. He had been watching his son's decline and suffering for many weeks, and had composure to commit his body to the earth, in sure and certain hope of a blessed resurrection. Mr. Need, Mr. Boyd, Mr. Fraser, and John were all who attended; they were all known to him since his arrival. . . . John left Kingston with a cold, and was very ill with fever during the journey, on which, from the state of the roads, he spent three days and three nights in reaching Peterboro. He took only one cup of tea during that time, and by total abstinence he thinks cured himself; but he became very thin.

The colony was at that time in an unsettled state with regard to education. The Act which had been passed by the Government had not given satisfaction, and the School Commissioners of the Fenelon district had come to no decision as to what course to pursue. Anne Langton was in doubt whether, in case there was no school established, she should resume her old labours,—try to establish a small school herself, or leave the young people to run wild for a time.

Extract from a letter from ANNE LANGTON *dated 16 May, 1842.*

We are just now enjoying the Canadian luxury of being without servant,—Margaret left us a week ago,—the article servant is scarce at present. Our neighbours are suffering in the same way. We are not quite so badly off when thus situated, for John's man's wife is at hand to apply to on emergencies. She comes up every evening to wash up, and on Saturday afternoon gives the kitchen a scrubbing. Our boy is rather much of a child, but perhaps all the better for that in the present state of the household, as he is not too proud yet to do a little woman's work when required, so that I hope we shall do pretty well until our enquiries are successful. John is at Peterboro at present, attending the second meeting of the District Council. We partly expect him home this evening, but not certainly, for the Council sat much longer last time. I mentioned in a former letter that the gentlemen of our district had declined to act as magistrates. The reason and motive of this action of theirs was to testify their disapprobation of the new appointments, make Government sensible of its blunder, and so lead to a speedy readjustment of things. The newly appointed magistrates were men of almost the lowest degree, some unable to sign their own names correctly, and utterly incompetent to perform the duties of their office. When John went recently to Ops about the robbery of the contents of our boxes, he had himself to draw out the warrant for the magistrate to sign, and to dictate in every particular what steps were to be taken, having in the first place lost time in seeking for another magistrate, because the one at hand, sensible of his own incompetency, had expressed reluctance to act.

Extract from a letter from ANNE LANGTON *dated 29 June, 1842.*

Our young men have decided to hold a ploughing-match this year with their horses and men. A field belonging to John is fixed upon for this trial of skill, and as the gentlemen will assemble we ask the ladies for the evening. After the labours of the day the men, and those in our immediate neighbourhood with their wives, are to have an entertainment in the barn, where music will be provided, and plenty of bun loaves, good rice-puddings, ginger-bread, and tea and coffee. I wish I could say no whiskey, but that cannot be omitted, as no temperance society is yet formed in this remote, uncultivated district. Our party mean to look in at them, and John will open the dance. It is the first agricultural meeting in this district. I am prepared with some beautiful pink ribbon to mark the winner. The gentlemen connected with the match will have the tent fixed on the hill for a cold dinner—and we shall entertain the ladies.

After Margaret left us we had the pleasure of remaining nearly five weeks without a servant at all—little Timothy excepted. Servants are very scarce just now. The people are becoming more independent of us, whilst we do not become more independent of them. None of the Peterboro servants will come so far back, so that beyond what the neighbouring townships offer there is small chance. How scarce girls are in these townships you may imagine when, among about fifty that we reckoned up of the neighbours to attend our entertainment next week, there will be only one unmarried girl, namely, our late servant, Sarah, about seventeen. However, we have at length succeeded in hearing of two servants, both new arrivals in the country, one the daughter of an Irish weaver, six-and-twenty, who has never been in service before. She is large and clumsy, very plain, and, I am afraid, rather stupid, but, as far as I can see, willing, so we must hope to make something of her. The other I know nothing of but that she is English, which sounds most promising in my mother's ears. Considering that we have the milk of eight cows to manage, and shall wash at home, I do not think the increase in our establishment too much.

As regards the school question, an Act had been passed by the Government in 1816 to establish and assist common schools in Upper Canada, and Commissioners appointed to enquire into the educational needs of the various districts. The Commissioners had decided against a school in Fenelon and Verulam, but as the inhabitants desired that their district should be made into a school district, they would have to pay a tax whether they had a school or not. A donation from the family at Blythe, who were anxious to have a school, and whose donation depended upon the establishment of one, turned the scale, and a school was started. The school had at first to be held in a barn temporarily, the small building used before in connection with the church not being available.

Extracts from a letter from ANNE LANGTON *dated 23 July, 1842.*

This sketch shows the scene of the ploughing-match, held on July 7. Right in the centre of the piece you see the roof of the barn in which the entertainment was held in the evening. A little to the left stands a beautiful marquee, surmounted by the British flag, and near it a group of ladies and gentlemen assembled to witness the spectacle. The dotted lines mark the land that was ploughed, and scattered up and down it you may perceive the four teams that contended for the prize. The one nearest this way, and now approaching the brow of the hill over which the barn is seen, is the one that will win the day. Beyond are seen the beautiful waters of Sturgeon Lake, and the woods and hills that surround it, and in the left corner you may observe another British flag floating over the residence of the Langton family. The whole thing went off very well, and occasioned less hurry and bustle than many a minor affair. We began in good time, and were baking every day for nearly a fortnight before, so that on the day itself, though we had to receive many of the gentlemen at breakfast and dinner, I felt perfectly at liberty to attend our lady guests when they began to arrive about three o'clock. Our party numbered twenty-six, and when after tea we joined those assembled in the barn I believe we were altogether about a hundred.

The ball was opened by a country dance, in which the gentry joined, and such of the people as were not too shy. These came out more in the jigs that succeeded, after which we gave them a quadrille, and then retired. We attempted no more dancing at the house, being scarce of young ladies, but had a very pretty supper, and when the ladies retired for the night some of the young men went down and had another fling in the barn, where the fun was kept up till after daylight. I am proud to say there was not a drunken man, except one of the musicians, who, although a temperance character, wet his lips too frequently with beer. An abundant supply of coffee and tea, and the milk of all the cows, preserved us from the disgrace which I had rather apprehended.

Some of the young men departed early, and we sat down only two-and-twenty to breakfast. Nine of the party we accommodated with beds in the house, the remainder rolled themselves in blankets, in the old backwoods style.[1] The entertainment in the barn being of far more importance than that here, I will tell you of what it consisted, in addition to the "Ram," an animal that was celebrated in the township, having in his day knocked down pretty nearly every man, woman, and child in it. There were twelve very large, cold rice-puddings, with abundance of currants in them; the same number of bun loaves, with eight or nine dozen of both ginger-bread cakes and of currant cakes, and plenty of bread and butter. In the meat line there was lamb and poultry, the garden and dairy furnishing a variety of accompaniments. We have estimated the expenses of this

[1] Note by John Langton—"Not one of us ever went to bed at all."

treat, and judge them to have amounted to £7: 10s., which I think it was well worth, from the great satisfaction it appears to have given in the neighbourhood. Perhaps that sum might not quite cover the wine and other extras here, but then we must have company sometimes.

Among the new arrivals is a medical man in Ops, who was summoned on occasion of a poor man's illness, and spent the evening with us. He appears a decent sort of person, and being within a few hours' call, may be a great acquisition in the neighbourhood, if he remains. The question is, whether he will be able to live upon our ailments.

John has to be very busy at present, for his man Henry is ill, and almost every day there is a "Bee" which takes every other hand away. These "Bees" are getting a perfect nuisance, the period between seed-time and harvest is almost filled up with them. Some of the gentlemen talk of forming a logging association, cutting "Bees" generally altogether, and helping each other with men and cattle for two or three days at a time. I do not know whether they will find this less inconvenient, but something of the kind is requisite where people have much land to log up, for it requires numbers to get on well and profitably.

I am sorry to tell you that we have another great bustle in prospect, nothing less than the taking down of both chimneys. We have been threatened with this necessity for some time, owing to their sinking. The builders up here were more inexperienced five years ago than they are now. The foundations were not well managed, and the chimneys themselves most enormous ones. Some of the rooms will be greatly improved by the alteration. One chimney we shall not rebuild, but have stoves. The horizontal lines of the building have been greatly unsettled by these weighty masses of stonework. . . .

John's present work is about as unpleasant as any that can devolve upon the Canadian settler. It is termed "branding" and consists in going about among the burning log heaps, and putting together the fragments as they scatter in burning down, so that all may be consumed. The heat, you may suppose, is just as much as is endurable. The smoke is most distressing to the eyes and the dirt beyond description. John has but a small piece of ground to burn himself, having given a job of clearing this year, but he has been "branding" the last three days, and it will take him at least another to get through. At night he goes to the lake to purify, but we admit him to the dinner-table in costume, the shades of which are somewhere between the smith and the chimney-sweeper.

I look with pleasure and admiration at our verandah when I take my morning walk in it. The vines are up to the ceiling, and one of the rose-trees (a wild one) is nearly as high, and is quite a picture, so covered with flowers, and giving a sweet perfume, the want of which I have felt in the flowers in general here. When I think of what we were four years ago, our progress about the premises is wonderful, and repays us for all our care and painstaking.

Extracts from a letter from ANNE LANGTON *dated 26 August, 1842.*

Can you fancy the interest and curiosity with which the little miniature cases were successively opened?[1] The representation of the one face we all perfectly know taught us in what respect we might, and in what we might not, trust to the correctness of the others. It was for the sake of the likenesses that we first contemplated them, and only subsequently as curious specimens of a new art. Nothing of the kind has been before seen up here, and by some who do not read newspapers as we do, not even heard of. Newspapers certainly do help to keep one a little *au fait* of what is going on in the world.

Extracts from a letter from ANNE LANGTON *dated 16 September, 1842.*

The last few weeks have been quite uneventful. John attended to his duties at Peterboro as Councillor and came home very disheartened about public business and the men

[1] Daguerreotypes.

he had to deal with. You must expect him to become very Tory-ish in his ideas. By a foolish Act, and a more foolish repeal of the same Act, they have thrown school matters again into confusion.

Our chief subject of interest lately has been a case of fever and distress in the neighbourhood. A man just come into the country died of fever. About a fortnight later three other members of the family fell ill. This occasioned a panic, and ended all but the most necessary intercourse with the shanties where the families lived. We had caused one of the two families living together to be removed to a shanty on our piece of land. One courageous woman has been invaluable in both places. She said that she smoked and before going into the house took a little brandy and wormwood and considered herself proof against infection.

Frost ought to be welcome this Fall, as it will probably prove a check to ague, which prevails still very generally, and there are still some other cases of fever in the neighbourhood. The Thornhill family who had been removed to our shanty are now all convalescent, and as no further fatal cases have occurred, I hope there is not so much danger in the present prevailing complaint as, from some of its violent symptoms, anxious friends are led to apprehend. We so often hear that people are not expected to live through the night that we begin to disbelieve the seriousness of the reports. They are very unknowing about medicines. Some take double doses, and our poor widow gave all the physic we sent to the one child who patiently took it, whilst the other who declined it went without. . . .

We killed a porcupine here the other day, and ate it. It is said to resemble sucking-pig, but I thought it more like lamb. We took good care to make away with its covering, for, alive or dead, they are very dangerous to the dogs.

Journal of ANNE LANGTON *for November, 1842.*

Tuesday, November 1. Our carpenter had to leave us in an unfinished state to go and get in his potatoes, but I am happy to say he is at work again now. The partition between the hall and dining-room is not yet up. The hall and dining-room will be heated by one stove, and the partition will be made to open with large doors if occasion requires it. A stove here is a perfectly movable piece of furniture, so that it may be placed elsewhere or taken altogether away, if in summer we were to desire to avail ourselves of the folding doors, and make a large room of the two. We are not contemplating giving a ball, but were pleased with the spacious, airy appearance, and the thing is easily done. The partition will be of butternut, and the dining-room will be lined with the same, but the hall will exhibit its bare logs for some time longer.

Thursday, November 3. The news of to-day is not very pleasant. The mill at the Falls is broken. However, as the accident by which it suffered might easily have proved fatal to two men, their escape should make us think more lightly of the minor evil. Nevertheless, the prospect of having to take every grain of wheat down to Bobcaygeon is dismal enough for the whole neighbourhood. We must eat less bread and more meat, which last is dreadfully cheap, so much so that nobody likes to kill anything that they can keep alive, and to make fat does not pay at all. Pork is something less than a penny a pound, and beef about a penny farthing.

Friday, November 4. John was at the Falls this morning and brought down the comfortable intelligence that the story about the mill is a great exaggeration, and that we may hope to have our corn ground as usual there this winter. His errand, in which he did not succeed, was to get a rafting-chain, having sent men to cut building logs a little lower down the lake, where they abound; and the woods around here have been well picked through. . . .

My mother's head continues very bad. John and I would persuade her that it is aguish. Everybody agrees that the headache which accompanies the prevalent complaint is very peculiar, and very bad; indeed it is attended with more, and more serious, aches and pains than I had conceived, and such as often occasion alarm until their connection with ague is clearly proved. I am strongly inclined to the opinion that ague was mingling itself with the late symptoms of my mother's illness last year. It is by no means necessary that a person must shake in the ague. When they do the complaint is more treatable; the dumb ague often lasts for months.

Sunday, November 6. Pretty busy we were giving John our list of commissions for Peterboro. It is a long one for he has not been down since the beginning of August, and will not go again, in all probability, during this year. Moreover, the Store at the Falls is now entirely given up, so that we have to send to Peterboro for every individual thing, down to a bit of pepper. I believe that Mr. Sawers intends to have a store at Bobcaygeon, but I do not anticipate much from it, nor can it be a great convenience to us.

Monday, November 7. I had a long confab with our school commissioner, Taylor, about the school. They are just beginning to build a house for it in a permanent situation, nearly three miles from here. I think I shall talk to Taylor about the library, as he is interested in all such things, and is the only active man in the Bobcaygeon library. I find that the quarterly sixpence is a hindrance to the circulation of the books. Some "intend" to subscribe and never do, whilst others who are really thriving say they have never found themselves rich enough. This must be more from the scarcity of cash than from the actual value of the sum. John says there seems no difficulty in producing sixpence for a glass of grog! I think I shall be obliged to accept a pound of butter or a few eggs in payment, and put the sixpence into the bag myself. I am afraid that I shall have to be perpetually dunning one subscriber or another. I talk as if I had a great many, but I have but four to my own library, and three to that of Bobcaygeon, some of them being the same.

Tuesday, November 8. I spent a great part of the morning in my store-room. You have no idea how things accumulate here. In the first place, there is the necessity of having stores of everything. Then there is the habit, that grows upon one, of having a good stock beforehand of consumables, and reserves of articles that are liable to decay, and lastly, the duty of carefully putting away anything that may by any chance ever become useful for any purpose again. If we send an order to the tailor we have to send thread, buttons, lining, etc., and sometimes the tailor will come to us to beg a bit of lining for another person's coat.

Wednesday, November 9. To-night I have been stitching very diligently at a gingham gown of my mother's that I am altering for myself; and when I have done it I must attack a silk one, which I consider a very important affair, for a better gown here lasts for years. The muslin one you got for me will last for ever, unless I degrade it. It has acted the part of a better gown a year and a half, that is, it has lain in my drawer ready for use, and has never been put on. This durability does not extend to common gowns, and I find my wardrobe suddenly getting low. If you see anything pretty for a morning gown I shall be glad if you will get it for me. When I say for morning I do not mean the rough garment I have described myself as wearing, but one in which I shall feel neatly dressed. I must tell you I grow more and more averse to light colours, and do not patronise thin muslins, because they look neat for so short a time. This will prove a very extravagant year, to make up for the last, when, beyond my English shoes, I spent nothing in dress, my mother having made me a present of the muslin, which she could well afford to do, as the sum total of her own expenditure had been eight shillings. There are certainly some advantages in living in the backwoods.

I am still more inclined to think that my mother's headaches are allied to ague, and could I disguise the bitter, I should be apt to put a dose of quinine in her coffee to-morrow morning. We were obliged to send for a collection of little phials of quinine, which are still in great circulation, and seldom a day passes that one does not appear to be replenished. I wonder how many doses of medicine I have weighed up in the last four months! I think almost as many as some village apothecaries.

Friday, November 11. If you have purchased any more stockings for me they will be welcome, as I care not how large is my stock of so useful an article. I intend to wear every one of those I have myself, they are very comfortable, now that I am accustomed to them. I believe I criticised the texture as well as the size, but I had been comparing them with some particularly soft ones of my mother's, of long ago, that I had been wearing. We had a fire in the hall stove for the first time to-day, when the dumb stove in my room was proved to give out a great deal of heat, and produced a most comfortable temperature. It is merely a sort of enlargement of the stove-pipe of sheet-iron, looks neat in the room, and will be a great addition to the comfort of the house. We are sadly spoiled in these cold winters with our heated halls and staircases, and fires in lodging-rooms from morning till night.

Monday, November 14. My mother has been amusing herself with making a warm petticoat for one of the family of the poor widow, whose case was mentioned in former letters.[1] Excepting for ague, which occasionally visits her, the family is quite recovered from sickness. We have had the old shanty made tight for her, so that she is as comfortably housed as many of her neighbours. A subscription list is now going the round. Some put down their names for a bushel of wheat, some for a small sum of money, or to such a value in provisions, and amongst us there will be no immediate prospect of starvation for her. Unfortunately the eldest girl, the only one old enough to be useful is exceedingly deaf, which will be a great hindrance to getting her into service. My mother talks of taking pains to make her a neat needlewoman which might compensate in part for her deafness.

1 See above, page 168.

Tuesday, November 15. My mother finds out that our life is dull now that she is not well, and as we have no prospect of visitors to enliven us it has been projected that I should go up to the Falls for our letters to-morrow, and try to bring home a little news, or variety of some kind, but there are many chances against my accomplishing the journey. John's non-appearance inclines me to believe that our information was erroneous, and that he has either gone to Cobourg, or has been otherwise detained on official business. He is in great hopes that he may be balloted out of the Council now. He neither likes the time it costs him nor the expense.

Thursday, November 17. I have been trying to manufacture myself a winter bonnet to-day, for I am getting tired of my cap. It is rather guess-work, as I am ignorant concerning shapes. However, I do not feel that it would be wise to send any order for a bonnet, as it is by no means every one that would suit my physiognomy. I wish that I could procure a Persian lady's head-dress, so as to conceal it altogether. Did we ever tell you that John one winter wore a black mask for the purpose of keeping his nose end warm?

Friday, November 18. Real winter at last, thermometer about 12, and a high wind. Many is the sigh that has been given to John to-day, wondering where he is, and wishing he were at home. But we in the house are not always good judges how endurable it may be outside. I remember feeling very anxious one day last winter, when he was to ride down to Peterboro, after staying the night at the Beehive, and consoling myself with thinking that he certainly never would set out, for it was as many degrees below zero as it is now above it, and blowing most fiercely, but he did set out, and, moreover, declared that he had never felt cold all day. I have completed my bonnet, and very pretty and snug it looks, that is, it would be pretty on any other head. I shall not want it till about Christmas, but I am getting all these little jobs done that I may with a good conscience make an attack upon my chair; it has been about nine months untouched.

Sunday, November 20. I hope the wind will not rise again to-night, for the sake of a basket of delicacies, which is doomed to pass it perched on the top of a high stump, if happily it does not lie at the bottom of it. My mother was sending an offering to Mr. Boyd, and Timothy, our boy, finding no one at home and the door locked, took this method of ensuring the safety of his cargo until Mr. Boyd's return; but it is scarcely likely that arriving at, or after, dark, the unexpected basket will attract his immediate attention. If it escapes the beasts of the field, there are the fowls of the air that might scent out the dainties. The thought of the feast they will have reminds me of one we saw devoured on the ice last spring. John had been observing the motions of an eagle, and, taking the telescope, saw it with its beak break through the ice, which must have been pretty thick, though softish, and afterwards with its talons hook on to a large muskinonge. We watched it for a long time enjoying its meal, whilst another eagle waited patiently to seize upon the remainder, when its companion should be satisfied, the smaller birds hovering round at a more respectful distance. The weather has been so moderate to-day that I think John may have set out, if his business was finished, but the character of the Cobourg discussion has been that of tedious delay all along. Moreover, he had another affair on hand besides the Council work, having been appointed an arbitrator in another dispute, the merits of which, nay, even the subject of it, he was unacquainted with when he went down.

Thursday, November 24. I am rejoiced to have to say that John is once more at home again. A bad cold had been the first cause of his detention, then unexpected public business, and these things, together with the inclemency of the weather and the dreadful state of the roads, combined to prolong his absence. John was strongly recommended and urged to come by Mud Lake and cross the ice. He entirely declined doing so; the same day a man was drowned in attempting it. Mr. Boyd, who was always a favourite, has completely won our hearts by paying us another visit. He brought back our empty basket, and alas! empty it had been when he found it the same morning. The united wisdom of our man and his man has not shone forth conspicuously. Why did not the former put his charge into the stable when he found the house shut? But the latter actually saw the basket on the stump an hour or two after it had been deposited there, and thinking it might be one of their own baskets, or perhaps not thinking at all, left it where it was. I must give you a specimen of simplicity in a daughter of the woods. In coming up John had followed a wrong track, and come upon a clearing that he was unacquainted with. Seeing a girl of about thirteen, he asked her whereabouts he was. Finding her puzzled to make a reply, he inquired who lived there. Her answer was "Father." "And who is your father?" This quite perplexed her, so he put his question in another form, "What do they call your father?" "Us calls him pa," was the most satisfactory information he could obtain, and he had to proceed to the house itself with his inquiry.

Friday, November 25. I forgot to acknowledge the receipt of your letter of October 16, and Mrs. Weld's, with the long recipe for currant wine, which at first sight quite frightened me, but I find it has acquired its magnitude from the character of the writer.

Monday, November 28. Mr. Boyd arrived again yesterday to pay his visit of welcome to John as he had of charity to us, and we have succeeded in keeping him to-day. Such a thing in ordinary times is a perfect impossibility, for he is one of the most industrious home-keeping settlers we have. But the snow has left him nothing to do, and I think if it does not go away, and make chopping practicable, we may have more of his company this winter than usual. The mercury has been dropping below zero, I suspect, though it was a trifle above it when I looked out this morning, and the putting-in of double windows, and stuffing with cotton-wool, has been a good part of my occupation to-day. One of the things that were not accomplished before winter set in was the erection of a new poultry-house. You know the cause of the evacuation of the old one. Their temporary habitation is found quite insufficient to shield them against the cold; one or two have had their feet frozen already, so we have sent them down to the farm-yard to sleep with the cattle. It is a very common thing for poultry to lose some of their toes in winter, and during the last one our cat lost a great part of one ear.

Tuesday, November 29. John will be away, I am afraid, for some weeks after the New Year. One arbitration comes on the beginning of January, the other towards the end of that month, and the District Council again early in February. Mr. Need was balloted out; John was not so fortunate. Mr. Need's deafness, which is much increased, makes him very unfit for the post of Council man.

Wednesday, November 30. Mr. Boyd left us this morning, and I do not think that John would have enjoyed his society much had he remained another day, for John is suffering to-night from rheumatism in his head, *alias* ague. I slipped away, unknown to him, after tea, and down to his house to put up his winter canopy, for the winds find such ready entrance into his house that such a shelter is quite necessary. I wished it had been fixed up sooner. When he is not well it is very dismal turning him out at nights, but he is very averse to leaving his own house, even for a time. We have had more snow, and the wind drifting it, so that the pathway was quite invisible, and I have seldom floundered through deeper drifts than to-night.

John is better this morning. Two applications for quinine convince us that ague is still stirring, notwithstanding the frost. This is unusual, and Canadians say that the species of ague we have had this year is much worse than ordinary ague. Some attribute it to the raising of our waters, and say we shall always have it; others assure us that everywhere it has been more prevalent than usual this year, so we hope to fare better another year. My mother's headaches continue, though not so severe, at least not so incessant. Aunt Alice is about middling.

Friday, December 2. There is a pile of hams and bacon ready for salting to-morrow, which looks like anything but a famine, but the larder presents a very different spectacle to what it did last year. There is neither beef nor mutton, the remains only of one solitary haunch of venison; nor have the woods furnished us with either pigeons or partridges this year, but there is plenty of pork.

Saturday, December 3. Once more I must take my leave of you, having now completed the twelfth journal. I can scarcely believe that I have given you the record of a whole year—at different times. You will see that times are somewhat changed since I commenced these scribblings. Many things are more complete and comfortable around us, and though some things are taken off our hands by the increase of our establishment, yet there remain an abundance of cares and occupation. The details I have entered less into than formerly, for there is much sameness in them.

1843

Extracts from a letter from ANNE LANGTON *dated 11 February, 1843.*

We have had a stirring time since our last letter left a week ago. On Sunday a party of Dunsfords, three gentlemen and Miss Dunsford, went up to church to take their guest, Miss Clarke, to Mr. Fidler's, and after leaving her there drove down with us to dinner before going home. Such a peppering storm of wind and snow had overtaken us that we did not let them proceed, and the weather continued so bad that they all remained with us until Tuesday. On that day John went down to meet and bring up Mr. Need, who had promised us a visit, and shortly after they had appeared two other gentlemen arrived, strangers, one personally, the other entirely. Of this last we should yet have known nothing but the name, Keeting, had not Mr. Need whispered that he was an Indian Chief. He was a thorough Englishman, nevertheless, but he had married a Chief's daughter, was adopted by him, and was now himself Chief of the tribe, and at present on an expedition amongst the Indians. We soon found that he was intimately acquainted with the Indians and their language, but so he was also with other peoples and their languages, being evidently a traveller, and a man of the world. His conversation was very amusing, and you may suppose in quite a different style from what proceeds from the Canadian farmer, engrafted upon the schoolboy, and of this last class are most of our young men.

All these remained with us until Friday, when John ac-

companied them down, as he had to go to Cobourg again
before the meeting of the Council.

The roads have been good for sleighing, and I made
my *début* in driving the other day. John had more grist
for the mill than he could take at once, so I volunteered
to drive one load, whilst he drove the other. Our journey
was performed very prosperously. A strange, luminous appearance in the heavens has been seen by many at different times lately. John saw it twice while on his travels—a
streak of light following the sun, neither resembling a
comet nor zodiacal light. We have no wise men here to
interpret it.

We have had a beautiful spring. The enormous quantity
of snow which remained undiminished until after April
had begun, disappeared rapidly by evaporation with much
less inconvenience than it usually gives, and since its
departure there has scarcely been a day when the business
of the garden has been interrupted by weather. I am sorry
to say that the ague prevails again, and the applications
for quinine are as numerous as ever. Our household,
once unsettled, continues so at present. Neither Margaret's
successor nor Timothy's are likely to remain. We intend
to do without a boy this summer, and share with John in
a man who is already somewhat known to us, and who may
accomplish the little work we have about the house at this
season without greatly interfering with his farm duties.
Margaret was married in March, and since her husband
took Mr. Boyd's farm he has lost twenty-one head of cattle,
counting lambs, so they have not begun their married life
prosperously. John's ewes, though never pinched for food,
had scarcely any sustenance for their offspring, so the
lambs have fared badly. We took one little lamb to rear,

which has been a source of interest and amusement the last month, and is now a wonderful pet. Aunt Alice is mourning over the disappearance of our cat, who, I fancy, has taken to the woods, as cats often do here. Mr. Boyd has had one nine years, which goes away every summer, and never shows itself until the approach of winter, when it returns as tame as ever, and takes to all its old habits again.

The visit of the Bishop was this year one of the principal events—for a confirmation. The little church at Fenelon Falls was not yet consecrated, owing to some difficulty about funds. The church at Peterboro was likewise in difficulties, and there was a possibility that it might be shut up.

Extract from a letter from ANNE LANGTON *dated 18 November, 1843.*

We had some visitors during October—three of the Miss Dunsfords among the number. Now winter has taken us rather by surprise. Of Indian summer we have not had a day this year, and very little fine weather since the first departure of summer.

The Falls is rather a melancholy looking place at present, so many families that had settled there gone.

Wolves are very numerous this winter. They have visited our flock twice, and our neighbours do not fare better. We had a daylight exhibition of them the other day. We observed five or six, and watched them through the telescope, sporting most composedly in the meadow for at least half-an-hour.

In December the principal event was the cutting of a new road to Bobcaygeon, which would greatly facilitate the necessary journeys to Peterboro, and make travellers independent of the condition of the lake.

Letter from JOHN LANGTON *to* WILLIAM LANGTON, *December 1843.*

They have handed over to me this letter which I will

begin with a continuation of a conversation I have just
been holding with Anne, the subject of which will no doubt
rather surprise you, being no less than an idea of my
going into Parliament. I have for two years heard rumours
of such a thing and have been frequently sounded upon
the subject by people from various townships, but I have
never distinctly as yet said yes or no upon the subject.
But I must soon, and probably even before I can hear
from you, come to some decision upon the subject as the
present Government is about expiring and during the winter
probably the candidates will be in the field. We are here
rather curiously situated with respect to our representation.
We formerly belonged to the County of Durham in the
Newcastle District and the other half of that district was
comprised in the County of Northumberland. At the Union
when the representation was altered and curtailed we had
not as yet been erected into a new District and Durham
returned one member while Northumberland was divided
into two ridings, the northern of which was identical with
the eastern half of our new District of Colborne, so that
when the new Act came into operation instead of the Colborne District being represented by one member, half of
it returned one and our half was still part of the County
of Durham for election purposes. This state of affairs being
favourable to the Radicals they have been in no hurry
to change it, but I understand we are likely to be now
taken away from Durham and added to the north riding
which will then be identical with the county of Peterborough and District of Colborne. It is only on this sup-
position that I should in any case come forward, but if
such is the case I probably may. There certainly is no
resident in our part of the District who would have nearly
as good a chance as I should, and we form nearly one-half
of the County and nine-tenths or more are Conservatives.
In the north riding where the Radicals are of some force
I am not so much known, but in two or three of the most
influential townships I am, and it is from them principally
that I have received requests to come forward. Besides

myself I hear of no less than five persons mentioned on the Conservative interest and one on the Radical, and if all the five come to the poll no doubt the Radical will get in and the Conservatives here are not wise enough to see this. My own opinion is that not one of the five will ever succeed even if they do not divide the interest, for not one of them has many active friends and many have on personal grounds most bitter enemies. I on the contrary have no enemy that I know of except our present Radical member, and I entertain very little doubt that if I come forward I shall be elected. Against one Conservative candidate the Radicals would not have a chance, and I certainly should not allow myself to be named unless the Conservatives are somewhat united. The principal question is as to the policy of going into Parliament at all, and here I am a good deal at a loss. As to expense, that is not much, for the new election laws have rendered it almost impossible to spend money on the occasion. The polls are held in the several townships and are to be kept open one day, and there are such stringent regulations to prevent treating, conveying electors to the poll, and even flags and music, that it will require a few years' experience before means of evading them are devised. The principal and almost only expense will be travelling about canvassing and that cannot be much where people put up at private houses oftener than at taverns. As to the expense of attending Parliament that is paid by a wage of $3.00 per day. The neglect of one's own business too will not be much, for our Parliaments do not sit long, and that in a vacant time of year. But what advantage is to be obtained by it? I am not gifted with any particular eloquence or genius for statesmanship so as to be either very useful or ornamental to the country, or to be likely to gain any important worldly advantage by becoming a public character, and it is hard to say what gain I might make by it. I put out of the question entirely the benefit which the public might receive from my presence in the legislature, as I suppose that would not be of any great moment. I am now only looking upon it from a personal point of view, and though I cannot see any great good to follow, I see no harm, and unless a man has some chance of mixing more in the world than I do, of knowing and being known, of hearing and being heard of, he may remain all his life in that most unpromising situation—a gentleman farming in Canada. I should like to hear your opinion upon the subject even should I have acted before receiving it, and when you do write you may spare yourself the trouble of giving me a lecture upon want of patriotism and interested motives etc., as I can easily conceive all that. I am not asking you advice as to the public advantage of going into Parliament but consulting you whether in my circumstances it would be personally advisable. I have political and local reasons for wishing to have a say in the affairs of the Province, and I think that I should make as useful a member as some and certainly a better one than others of the candidates, but I should hardly be patriotic enough to entail upon myself the trouble, expense, and anxiety of public business unless I saw a probability at any rate of not injuring my own personal interests.

As to political matters in the Province they are in the very worst possible situation and must end, I think, in a separation of the Canadas or in another rebellion. Lord Sydenham was a real governor, and contrived to manage all parties and have his own way in spite of them all, and this is, I believe, the only way to keep matters smooth here. As long as we are a Province we must accommodate ourselves to the policy of the Home Government of which the Governor is the organ. If a few leading demagogues, backed by a temporary majority, are to lead the Governor by the nose, and he is to be allowed no resistance, we cease to be a Province and become an independent State, which God forbid! Lord Durham's system of Responsible Government takes all power away from the Governor to place it in the ministry, and for any good he might, as far as I can see, as well have remained in Downing Street. Lord Sydenham put his own interpretation upon the matter, which agreed also with Lord John Russell's, and he was by no means a cipher, but oddly enough the Tories have allowed, or at least tacitly allowed, the full democratic extent of responsibility, and their Governors have done neither good nor bad, simply nothing. I cannot help thinking that this apparent supineness on the part of the Government at home is a deep policy after all. They perhaps mean to let the Radical party have their full swing until by their overbearing triumph, their reckless tampering with all our old institutions, their favouring of the French rebels, and their undisguised democratic policy they have disgusted all the moderate and British population, and then perhaps they hope to be better supported in re-establishing something like a constitutional form of government. If such is their meaning I doubt its wisdom, though the present ministry have already excited plenty of that disgust; but things were to begin with in a very satisfactory state when they sent out that old woman Bagot. If they mean things to continue as they have gone on for the last year or two they may as well give up Canada at once. However, we will hope for the best. The Governor and his ministry have at last split, though upon what point we do not as yet know in this remote corner of the world, and as the elections will soon be coming on I hope and believe that the people, of Upper Canada at least, will show them that they mean to be governed on British principles. I must stop to catch the post.

1844 — 1846

Notes from letters written during 1844.

In February Anne Langton paid a visit to the Beehive to officiate as bridesmaid at Caroline Dunsford's marriage to Mr. Boyd, and remained there a couple of days after it, her mother and aunt, she says, rather enjoying the novelty of being left to themselves. Some efforts were made to get rid of the wolves which haunted the clearings this winter. Unfortunately the lamb, which had been made such a great pet, disappeared one morning, and though followed by its tracks a few minutes later, had evidently gone to meet a wolf under the impression that it was one of the dogs, and had fallen a victim.

There were many changes among the old original settlers at this time, either by their abandoning their farms in despair of making them lucrative, and taking to other occupations, or by leaving the country altogether. The immediate neighbourhood of Blythe was somewhat deserted this year. The Wallis's and Dennistouns were living at Peterboro, Mr. Dundas had obtained an appointment from the Hudson's Bay Company, and others were on the move. Mr. Need went to England at last, after much indecision.

There was much complaint about the mismanagement of the post-office department. Letters had been frequently lost owing to incapable and unreliable postmasters. This state of things was particularly felt at Blythe, owing to the anxiety about the health of the brother in England, who had gone early in the years to Italy for a few months. The letters from the Continent were especially interesting to

185

Anne, recalling, as they did, recollections of their sojourn there in their young days.

Towards the end of the year ague attacks were frequent, and more or less acute. A sufferer describes the mysterious illness as sudden and unaccountable. One day he would be perfectly delirious, with fever, acute headache, pain in the back and in all the limbs, the next going about his work apparently quite well, after an attack of violent perspiration. The next day again, he would be almost unconscious of what was passing around him. Recovery was usually quick, and the symptoms of "shaking," supposed to be an invariable accompaniment, by no means so.

Extract from a letter from JOHN LANGTON.

I am afraid that our neighbours are a great plague to you. I know they are to me. When it is known that I am going to Peterboro you would be astonished at the levees which I hold. One wants a pound of tea, another two yards of flannel, a third a pair of shoes, with some incomprehensible peculiarity about the instep. The tea is not to be of the same kind as one of the two dozen different parcels which I brought out five months ago. I am to get a reduction on the flannel, because the calico I brought last spring was of bad quality. One man wants a slate pencil, for which he duly deposits a half-penny, and another gives seven-pence halfpenny on account of his pound of tobacco; but the shoes, the flannel, the axe, and the sugar-kettle are sure to be on "tick." If John Bull's idea of paradise is, as Sydney Smith says, a land of short credit and cash payments, I should strongly recommend John Bull to stay at home.

Extract from a letter from ANNE LANGTON *dated Peterboro, 10 January, 1845.*

I came down to stand godmother to Mr. Wallis's little boy, Henry Alexander. The ceremony took place yesterday. We had a sleigh-drive in the afternoon. The day was beautiful, and I scarcely think that in Maderia you would be enjoying a milder air, and certainly not a brighter sun.[1] My time has been fully occupied with shopping and driving—very pleasantly, but I shall be very happy to get home again.

I am amused by the needless pity bestowed upon us by the people here, who evidently think the selection of the woods something very dreadful. We had a gay and busy Christmas —contrary to expectations—and a large party on Christmas Day. Mr. Need brought a young friend.

I went with some of the party to the Beehive, where the New Year was brought in with singing and dancing.

In a letter of February 17, John announces his engagement to Miss Lydia Dunsford.

The marriage took place on May 8—a quiet family wedding—the brothers of the bride rowing the newly-married couple from the Beehive up to Blythe. Aunt Alice had been hoping that the wedding would be fixed for the 27th—the anniversary of the marriage of her father and mother, just one hundred years before, in 1745; but it was not found convenient. Mr. and Mrs. Dunsford had lately moved to Peterboro, leaving the eldest son, James, in possession of the Beehive, with a sister.

The society on Sturgeon Lake was at the time greatly reduced—Mr. James Dunsford and Mr. Boyd alone remaining. The Hamiltons and others were all dispersed.

From the journal of ANNE LANGTON *for April, 1846.*

Thursday, April 2. There is certainly no novelty in the opening of the month, for it has found me at the old employment of candle-making. The increased facility of John's machine made me think that it would be profitable to manufacture on a large scale instead of merely using up our own tallow, or an occasional cake purchased from a neighbour. So John brought me up 54 lbs. of tallow,

[1] William Langton was, with his wife and a daughter, spending the winter in Madeira for his health.

and I was pleased this morning after two days' work to weigh up 49 lbs. of candles, having 5¼ lbs. of tallow left. This business may account for my beginning my journal on the second instead of the first of the month.

This morning I made my first round of the garden to see what signs of life appeared there. Tulips and hyacinths are above ground in most places, and if this weather continues the garden will be ready for me before I am ready for the garden.

Friday, April 3. Rather an unsettled and busy day. Both the servants went to the Falls, and what with helping them on in the morning, and supplying their place in the afternoon, I was pretty well occupied. I could not help thinking how soon one unlearns a good lesson. Considering how often we have been without servants, as much as for five weeks at once, I thought a wondrous deal about baking bread and getting tea ready. It is to be hoped one would learn the good lesson again pretty easily if occasion required.

Monday, April 6. My mother a little better to-day, being relieved by sleep and perspiration, and well enough to take an interest in the day, and be anxious for rather a better dinner in honour of John's birthday. I did my best, therefore, on very small materials. The usual party on this day falls through for lack of numbers, for it is really no compliment to ask people to come over very bad roads, without either good company or a good dinner to offer, and this is the very worst season of the year to provide the latter. At present provisions are at their lowest ebb. We are without fresh meat, the pork is done, for as we overstocked ourselves last year, of course we rather understocked ourselves this year. We have no bacon but what is two years old, and this year's hams are most indifferent, owing either to impure salt or impure molasses, or some other unknown cause. In general we shine in this article, and we have a small reserve of better ones, which, being the only good thing in the house, we use carefully.

Milk and butter will not be plentiful for a month to come, eggs are our chief luxury, and with these we make as much variety as we can. After all, I suppose the scarcity of the season is not regarded so much by anybody except the housekeeper, whose ingenuity is tasked to spread a decent table before the family. Sometimes, on the contrary, we are oppressed by plenty, as, for instance, when we had six sheep killed at once. You will wonder why they are not killed off more by degrees. The fact was that the sheep were fat, and fodder much too scarce to keep them so, and I must say that the last joint of mutton was as good as the first. We had beef, veal, and poultry to dispose of at the same time. I must tell you that Mary weighed up 52 lbs. of nice fresh soap with as much pride as I counted over my candles, and indeed it is a much more satisfactory operation altogether. Soap-boiling approaches nearer to creating than anything I know. You put into your pot the veriest dirt and rubbish, and take out the most useful article.

Tuesday, April 7. I need not say more than that this was *washing day*, a word of most comprehensive meaning, well understood by all householders.

Friday, April 10 (Good Friday). We sometimes attempt to keep more plants in the house than we have good light for, nor can we secure for them an even temperature. My mother's rose-trees flourish better than anything else. I counted twenty-five buds and flowers in the drawing-room windows this morning.

Saturday, April 11. Mr. Wickham arrived in the evening, having been three days travelling up from Peterboro. Yesterday he was nearer home than he is now, but, finding bad ice where he had hoped to cross the lake, he was compelled to go all round by the Falls. As he stays the night here it will be the fourth day before he reaches home. This is just the season when we are the most perfectly quiet, as everybody stays at home that can do so.

Tuesday, April 14. The people are beginning to come

round with their sugar to sell, all wanting to get fivepence a pound for it, whereas fourpence has been the regular price the last year or two. I bought some to-day for fourpence halfpenny, and was amused with the gracious, flattering manner in which the man came down in his price, saying, "Well, I would not for a halfpenny give the sugar to anybody else if you wanted it." The sugar-making season generally brings us in some of our smaller debts. At present we have more than £80 owing to us, from loans and other things. Amongst these debts is the fortune of the little girl whose father was drowned in the regatta, and which has hitherto all come out of our pocket. This requires explanation, and the circumstances are illustrative of the state of things in this country. The collection was set on foot by Mr. Rubridge, and he in the first place received the money and the contents of the prize purse. A year or more passing without anything being heard of it, John, feeling that he had no more business than any other person to make an inquiry, told Jordan, the grandfather of the child, to write him a note requesting him to enquire about it, which note became his authority for doing so. Mr. Rubridge, on being asked, thought he had paid the money to Mr. Langton, but on further tasking his memory discovered that it was to Mr. Kirkpatrick. The lawyer present on the occasion, on application to this gentleman, found that at first he remembered nothing at all about it, but finally it was distinctly recalled to his recollection that he had received the money, but how much neither he nor anybody else could tell. To find out the sum was difficult; the subscription list was forthcoming, but everybody knew that it was quite common for names of persons to be put down who never paid. This was therefore no guide. Finally, Mr. Kirkpatrick agreed to consider it twenty-five pounds, and paid it by making over to John and Mr. Wallis, as trustees, two debts due to himself. Meanwhile John met with a single bank share, which is not often to be obtained, and he purchased it for the child, and we remained the creditors. How long we shall continue creditors remains to be seen. John succeeded in screwing ten dollars the other day out of one of the people, which is the first we have seen of the money owing.

Friday, April 17. I have been just called down to a little girl, who had brought back some sewing she had done for us, and for whom we feel much interested. Her mother died in her confinement last year, leaving this poor girl of ten years of age with several younger brothers and sisters to take care of. My mother paid for a six months' nursing-out of the little delicate baby, and it is now a thriving, healthy child. Another woman died under the same circumstances, literally of cold, and the baby was, while in the charge of another woman, found one morning outside the family group in bed, and frozen to death. This was on one of our coldest nights this winter.

Thursday, April 23. I suppose there is certain pleasure in communicating ill news (which may account for its flying so fast). I could be amused at the eager haste with which our maiden, Susan, reports any calamity to me, coming to my bedside, and rousing me to hear her news. This morning my awakening senses were greeted with, "Miss Langton, you know old Lansfield, well! he is drowned." Old Lansfield has a young wife and family. At present these tidings are mere report. It was once reported at Peterboro that John was drowned, and when he walked into the town he was stared at as if he had been a ghost. He had left Bobcaygeon in his canoe for Peterboro on a very stormy day, and had been met on his way thither. The wind at length became so strong that he was obliged to put his canoe to shore, in a part of it which made access to Peterboro not easy; so he crossed the woods to another township, where he had an acquaintance, and had to wait there two days before the storm subsided and he could pursue his journey. Meanwhile Mr. Need had gone down to Peterboro, and as John had not been seen or heard of, little doubt of a fatal catastrophe remained in the minds of any of his friends, who were accordingly preparing to seek for his body when he made his appearance.

Monday, April 27. The only interesting event to-day for me was the sight of an old pupil, grown into a man.

Wednesday, April 29. Yesterday I spent a good part of the day in gardening, and had to lament the demise of the lavender plant.

To-day being wet we devoted our energies to cutting-out work, of which there is plenty of one sort or another before us. There is bedding to be overhauled, pillows to fill, mattresses to take to pieces and remake, and a new one to manufacture. I well remember the last time we had this work to do. We were in the midst of hair and wool when our only servant fell ill, and besides the business on hand, and no assistance except that of a little girl, who was helping to pull the wool, we had the invalid to nurse and sit up with. It was a right busy time.

Notes from letters, May to September, 1846.

In May John took his wife to Peterboro for her confinement. During their absence began the terrible visitation of ague and fever, which was long remembered in the Lake district. New forest settlements are all subject to such visitations at a certain period of their history. The miasma is generated from decaying vegetation. When the forest is cleared to a certain extent, and sunshine is let in upon a sufficiently large tract of country, then the evaporation, which is comparatively harmless while under the shadow of its own woods, becomes baneful. Time only, with the increase of the area of cultivation, bringing purer air, can remedy the evil, and render the country again healthy. In the case of the district round Sturgeon Lake the evil was made worse by the fact that the waters of the lake had been raised by the construction of a dam and locks at Bobcaygeon. A great deal of land near the lake shores was submerged, so that in dry seasons, when the water was low, there was an immense amount of new decaying matter exposed to the sun. Two seasons of this state of things resulted in a visitation of ague intensified into fever. Of the Blythe party Anne was first taken ill, then her mother, on her eightieth birthday, July 25th. Already in feeble health, she succumbed to the fever, and died on August 1. John had, of course, returned to Blythe on hearing of his mother's illness. The harvest was coming on, and two friends came from Cameron Lake to assist him in getting it in, but before long all farm work had to be abandoned, all the men and their families being prostrated with either ague or fever.

Extracts from a letter from ANNE LANGTON *dated Thursday, 17 September, 1846.*

I am sorry to report that both Aunt Alice and I have the ague. My aunt has been very weak and ill the last few days, and I have apprehended something of this sort. It will be very trying to her, with the small amount of strength she has wherewith to combat disease. It is bad for us to fall ill together, but it would have been still more unfortunate had it happened last week, for our little maiden had the ague then.

John's man Henry's case was pretty severe, but he is now mending very nicely. The people generally look something like the poor wretches that thronged about us at Paestum—William will remember them, and I daresay you saw something of it in the fever districts in Italy. They say that there has not been such a year as this since the year 1827, when it was still worse. There have been more deaths on the other side of the lake. In some respects we are better off from having four families habitually provided with some medicines. In some settlements there is nobody near to apply to, and the poor creatures have nothing to do but lie down, and let the fever take its course. One widow woman, living alone, was found to have been dead two or three days by the neighbours.

The other man working here took himself off for fear

of infection. John had engaged this man to do his plough-ing, and the first thing he had to do was to take the horses a two days' journey to get shod, one blacksmith being laid up. Now he had just come home with the ague. Whole families are down with ague or fever, and perhaps no one to look after them but a neighbour, a mile away, herself in a state of ague. One great lamentation among the sick has been the difficulty of getting any washing done. John was called upon last week to read the funeral service, as Mr. Fidler had gone away for change of air. A great part of this month we have had extremely hot weather. However, I am thankful to say that the mosquitoes are all over. They have been a dreadful plague this summer.

Saturday, September 19. John went down to try to get our former servant, Margaret, but she had all her children ill. There is not a person anywhere around whom it is pos-sible to get. I took quinine to-day, but fear that it will not prevent to-morrow's visitation. As long as I am up I can look after Aunt Alice, and our young servant manages some way or other, but when I am down it is difficult for a girl of sixteen to do the churning, baking, washing, etc., and make tea and gruel every hour of the day.

John's new man is a decided case of fever, so here we have him to nurse for five or six weeks, I daresay. But what is worse Henry's wife, Angel Brandon, is beginning to be ill herself. She thinks it will only prove to be ague.

Now the last woman about the place is on the sick list, and it is much more difficult to let woman's work stand still than men's work. John had made up his mind that nothing could be done on the farm, but no bread! no butter! no clean clothes!—this is another matter.

JOHN LANGTON *adds:*

Although all this sounds very dreadful, it is astonish-ing how we keep our spirits. There is something absurd in the very inconveniences which we are exposed to. The idea of Billy and me having to cook, milk the cows, etc., and attend upon two men, five women, and three children, all more or less ill of ague and fever, has a good deal of the ludicrous in it. The thing that now most alarms me is that I only know in this neighbourhood three men who would be able to take a boat down to Peterboro, and if I get ill, and Lydia has to be sent for to nurse us all, what am I to do if those three last hopes fall ill too! We will hope for better times.

The day after this letter was concluded—on September 20—Miss Currer's strength gave way suddenly, and she died, just six weeks after her sister. She was laid to rest in Fenelon churchyard, on September 22, and a few days later Anne left Blythe for the very necessary change of air and scene. She went to Peterboro, where, until the middle of October, she was the guest of her friends, Mr. and Mrs. Wallis. John followed her later when the invalids about the place were sufficiently recovered to allow of his leaving them, and in October they all returned to Blythe for the winter. `

In June, 1847, they sailed for England, John and his wife to return after a short stay of three weeks, Anne to remain for nearly three years.

EPILOGUE

It may be that some who have read the foregoing letters from the backwoods would like to know what the future had in store for the two survivors of the Langton family, Anne and John. The death of the father, within a year of his venturesome expedition to join his son, had not caused any change of residence for the three ladies to be even suggested. The family had left England to join the younger son in Canada who was unmarried and alone, and it had been considered best that they should come and help him rather than remain in England where the elder son, married and with a growing family, had no such pressing need of companionship. The father's death made no difference in the position. John was still alone and as much in need of female assistance and sympathy as before. He now moved definitely from his own small log cabin and joined the three ladies in the Blythe house. But in 1845 he married, and brought his wife to share the Blythe home with his mother, aunt and sister, and for more than a year they all lived together with great mutual affection. This happy family was broken up in the late summer of 1846 by the successive deaths, within six weeks, of the mother and the aunt, and Anne decided that she would now return to England, for a time at least, being no longer necessary to her brother John as a housekeeper. So the letters from Anne to the brother in England, which are printed in this volume as descriptive of the settler's life, came to an end.

John also had, from time to time, written letters to his brother, discussing his difficulties and getting advice. He had become increasingly interested in public affairs and was recognized as a leader in township matters. In 1840 when a militia regiment was embodied in the district he became one of the captains and mustered his company at Eldon. In a letter of May, 1841, he speaks of a journey to Peterborough with Mr. Need for the purpose of advocating at a public meeting the construction of locks at Bobcaygeon, and perhaps at Fenelon Falls likewise, which would facilitate communication by steamboat among the upper lakes. This was part of the ambitious project called the Trent Valley Canal, which was expected to provide a complete waterway from Lake Huron to Lake Ontario, superseding the long roundabout voyage by Lake St. Clair, Lake Erie and the Welland Canal. Then in the latter part of 1841 he had been appointed by the government a member of the District Council for Fenelon, in the hands of which all the management of local affairs was placed, including the maintenance of schools. In February, 1844, he wrote a long letter to his brother describing the financial difficulties of the Council and his exertions in overcoming them. Later he became Warden, as the chairman was called. This District business, as well as other private matters, had taken him frequently to Peterborough where he now had a good many intimate friends, Wallis, Dennistoun, Hamilton, and others. Through their efforts perhaps, it was proposed that he should be asked to become a candidate for election to the Parliament of the province at the election which was to be held in 1844. This proposal he discussed at great length in a letter of December 1843, speaking very modestly of his own value as a legislator and debater, and setting forth what he considered the advantages and disadvantages to himself of a political career. But when the promised election was held in 1844 he had declined to accept a nomination. In 1851, however, as will be mentioned later, he did allow himself to be brought forward as a candidate and was elected, and the whole course of his life was altered thereby.

In the meantime other events of importance had taken

place. He had married in 1845 and this additional responsibility stimulated his efforts to find some occupation more
lucrative than farming. Even before his marriage he had
written a letter (Oct. 21, 1844) discussing various ways
of making money in conjunction with the farm. A distillery,
to turn to account surplus grain, and a store in connection
with the distillery, a steamboat to ply on the lakes, provided
that the lock at Bobcaygeon was finished, successively engaged his attention. He even contemplated entering the
legal profession, although this would involve separation
from the farm, for he declared that as soon as admitted to
practice as barrister and solicitor he would establish himself at once in Toronto, to which all the really important
legal business was taken.

In 1845 his marriage occupied his mind and likewise
an epidemic of fever and ague, which seems to have been
caused by the unhealthy swamps left when land was partially cleared for farming, and fallen trees choked the small
streams draining the land. Both of the older ladies were
seriously ill, but recovered during the summer. Next year,
however, there was a more serious and wide-spread visitation of fever, and the Langton household lost both mother
and aunt. Anne herself was very ill at the same time and
after the second funeral was sent to the Wallis household
at Peterborough to recuperate, while John and his wife
likewise made a long stay in the same place with their
Dunsford relatives. In 1847 John and his wife as well as
Anne paid a visit to England. During this visit John was
strongly urged by his brother to abandon Canada and
return to England for good. The influence which William
could exert in financial circles, being at this time Manager
of the Heywood Brothers Bank in Manchester, would
ensure some position being found for his brother, and the
latter's experience, industry, and financial talent would
make his future career a success. John, however, after some
deliberation, decided against abandoning Canada and
Blythe. Fourteen years of the settler's life, hard though it
had been and disappointing as to its profit, had attached

him to the colony, and he never regretted his decision to remain in Canada to the end.

John and his wife returned to their home on Sturgeon Lake after only three weeks in England, but without Anne. The visit of the latter originally intended to be for one year, was gradually extended as more and more invitations from relations and friends were pressed upon her, and, as her sketch-books reveal, not only many parts of England were visited, but also Ireland, Wales and Jersey. A proposition had also been made to her by an old friend, Miss Lowe, to become an assistant mistress in a school for girls which the Lowe sisters had established at Mayfield, near London. In later years this school became well known, and pupils were sent to it even from Canada. The idea of becoming a schoolmistress was by no means displeasing to Anne and she had already practised the art in a small way on Sturgeon Lake among the children of the settlers about Blythe. But she finally decided that her real sphere of usefulness would be with the brother in Canada where a young family would be growing up. The enthusiastic letters which she received from her brother and sister-in-law in expectation of her return to them confirmed her in this decision. So in June 1850 she returned to Canada and to the Blythe household.

Blythe was still the home, although business affairs were drawing John to Peterborough. In 1849 he had become a partner of his brother-in-law, Mossom Boyd, in the lumber trade. Farming alone was not sufficiently profitable for the new demands upon him as the father of a family. But trade was bad, and lumbering was a hazardous speculation. His health, moreover, at this time was a cause of anxiety. Some affection of the throat had attacked him, and during 1850 he suffered a good deal and made several visits to New York for expert medical advice and treatment. So he withdrew from the partnership with Boyd whose tremendous energy was then laying the foundation of the highly successful business of later years.

The outcome of the treatment by New York doctors

was complete restoration to health, and in 1851 he was persuaded to become a candidate for Parliament to represent the County of Peterborough, and was elected. This new development made it expedient that the household should move to Peterborough, so Blythe was given up, although the farm was retained for the present, and hopes no doubt were entertained for an eventual return to the delights of a country life. Having moved to Peterborough, Langton looked about for further occupation and became the owner of certain mills near by, which he hoped might become a profitable investment. They never did, and in 1854 were given up.

As a member of Parliament, the Parliament of the united provinces of Upper and Lower Canada, his duties took him to Toronto for a part of every year, and he soon became recognized by his party leaders as a man to be considered.

There was a story current some years ago among his surviving contemporaries that a financial difficulty which had arisen between the Canadian and British Governments had to be explained to the Canadian Parliament. It was a matter of some intricacy and the explanation presented by the Finance Minister broke down under the impact of questions which he was unable to answer. Then Langton, who had listened attentively to the statement, got up and said that he saw an explanation of the difficulty that had arisen, and offered his suggestion to the Minister and the House. He succeeded not only in making clear what the Minister himself had not fully understood, but in so impressing the Government leaders that when it became necessary for an Auditor General of Public Accounts to be appointed as a permanent official they were agreed at once in offering the post. The letter from Macdonald in which the offer is made was dated February 6, 1855, and is printed in *Early Days in Upper Canada*. To accept would mean abandonment of all political ambition and would also put an end to all actual contact with Sturgeon Lake and Blythe. He would henceforth have to live in Toronto or

Quebec or wherever else the government offices would be. On the other hand it would put an end to his financial anxieties. He was now 47 years of age and had a family of five children. The future of this young family must be made secure. So he accepted the position but it was not until November that he entered upon his duties. Meanwhile he moved his household to Toronto. Blythe and the farm were sold and city life began.

While living in Toronto Langton found a new interest. This was the welfare of the University of Toronto which had been reorganized on a non-sectarian basis by Acts of Parliament, in 1850 and again in 1853. The governing body was the Senate, to which the Provincial Government had the right to appoint a majority of the members. Others were representatives of University College, which was the teaching authority as the Senate was the examining and degree-conferring body. Other members would be representatives of the rival universities. The Senate elected a Vice-Chancellor as its chairman and executive officer. Over all was the Provincial Government which controlled the endowment and administered the finances through its officer, the Bursar. As a sign of the Government's supremacy the Lieutenant-Governor held the honorary, but sometimes (as it turned out) influential, position of Visitor. The Chancellor was a representative of the graduates elected by them in Convocation. He was an honorary member of the Senate but otherwise without duty to perform except the conferring of degrees at the annual Commencement. Langton, being a Cambridge graduate, was considered to be a suitable member of the Senate and was appointed to it as one of the Government members in 1853. He soon became interested, and was strongly opposed to the party which aimed at a division of the endowment among the so-called universities of the respective denominations. The Church of England had been ousted from its control of the state university and Bishop Strachan had obtained funds in England to enable him to establish Trinity College. The Presbyterian Church had its own Queen's University at

Kingston, and the Methodist Church had Victoria College at Cobourg. All these forces were combined to induce the Government to divide the endowment of the provincial university on the plea that each of them was contributing to the higher education of the province as much at least as was the so-called provincial and "Godless" university. It did not require much penetration to see that local and personal considerations would be likely to prevail in these sectarian colleges over the claims of scholarship. The professional members of the Senate, Wilson, Croft, Cherriman, became intimate friends with Langton, who was elected Vice-Chancellor in 1855. He soon was engaged in controversy with the denominational partisans, of whom the chief was the Reverend Egerton Ryerson, at that time Superintendent of Education, there being no Minister as yet. A reference of the endowment questions to a Committee of the Legislature brought out such forcible and convincing arguments from Professor Wilson and the Vice-Chancellor that the demand for disendowment was refused. But everybody knew that the defeat was only temporary and that the demand would be renewed. Then there came into Langton's mind the idea that a building of monumental proportions and of capacity sufficient for a hundred years of growth would establish the non-sectarian provincial college beyond the possibility of destruction, and would also absorb so much of the endowment as to render the remainder less desirable to the other colleges, for these would probably have to submit to some measure of government inspection and control if they accepted any such financial assistance. In this project Langton received enthusiastic support from the official Visitor, Sir Edmund Head, who had a passion for handsome buildings. The whole story of the building, begun in 1856 and completed in 1858, is told in *Early Days in Upper Canada* in the letters written by John to his brother in November 1856. It is sufficient here to say that this masterstroke of policy was carried out in two years, and served to lay the spectre of disendowment for nearly thirty years, when it reappeared under the name of University Federation and finally prevailed.

To resume the history of Langton's life, the change in the seat of Provincial Government from Toronto to Quebec in 1859 put an end to the Toronto residence, and a new home was found in Quebec which was maintained until 1864, and another for two years more at Pointe Lévis. By that date the terms of the new Canadian Confederation had been practically settled, the new capital, Ottawa, had been accepted, permanent office buildings were erected there, and the Auditor-General moved his family from Quebec in 1866. From that date until his superannuation in 1878 he remained in Ottawa, a hard-working official. For what he accomplished in practically creating his department reference may be made to an article by H. R. Balls in the *Canadian Historical Review* for 1940, entitled "John Langton and the Canadian Audit Office." The difficulties which he encountered, both from the spending departments which disliked his insistence on account-keeping and faithfulness to the terms of the appropriations made for them, and likewise from the vacillation of Finance Ministers, are given in letters written from December 30, 1855, to November 12, 1856. (*Early Days in Upper Canada*, pp. 217-273). On his retirement he moved his household again to Toronto, where his eldest son was already established as a lawyer and where he still had many old friends. In Toronto he died, March 19, 1894.

The later history of Anne Langton was uneventful except for moving from place to place as a member of John's household. She did indeed visit England many times during this period; her last transatlantic journey was in 1879. As her deafness increased with age she depended more and more on her art for interesting occupation. There survive many admirable paintings of hers, some of Italian scenes, a panorama of the river St. Lawrence above and below Quebec, accepted by the Archives Department at Ottawa as a valuable historical record. Sketches of Ottawa and its neighbourhood are similarly of historical value as showing its appearance between 1870 and 1880. When too old for out-of-doors sketching she took to china painting, and thus maintained her artistic interest to the end. But the real purpose of her later life was to be useful to her brother's family, and her success was marked, for to all of them she seemed a second mother, ever interested, helpful, and devoted.

INDEX

Books in the Clarke Irwin Paperback series: